# Anne Bogart
## VIEWPOINTS

Anne Bogart is Co-Artistic Director of the Saratoga International Theater Institute (SITI) which she founded with Japanese director Tadashi Suzuki in 1992. She is a recipient of two Obie Awards and a Bessie Award and is an Associate Professor at Columbia University. Recent productions include *Small Lives/Big Dreams*, derived from the five major plays of Anton Chekhov, created with the SITI company; *The Medium*, an original work based on the theories of Marshall McLuhan performed in Japan, Saratoga Springs, and the New York Theatre Workshop, created with the SITI company; *Marathon Dancing* by Laura Harrington at En Garde Arts; *Escape From Paradise* by Regina Taylor at Circle Repertory Theatre; *The Women* by Clare Boothe Luce at Hartford Stage; William Inge's *Picnic* at Actors Theatre of Louisville; *Behavior in Public Places*, based on the theories of Erwin Goffman produced by Via Theater; Charles L. Mee, Jr.'s *Orestes* with SITI in Japan and Saratoga Springs; *American Vaudeville*, created with Tina Landau at the Alley Theater in Houston; Paula Vogel's *The Baltimore Waltz* at Circle Repertory Theatre and Bertolt Brecht's *In The Jungle of Cities* at the New York Shakespeare Festival.

**Smith and Kraus** *Books For Actors*

## MONOLOGUE SERIES
The Best Men's / Women's Stage Monologues of 1993
The Best Men's / Women's Stage Monologues of 1992
The Best Men's / Women's Stage Monologues of 1991
The Best Men's / Women's Stage Monologues of 1990
One Hundred Men's / Women's Stage Monologues from the 1980's
2 Minutes and Under: Character Monologues for Actors
Street Talk: Character Monologues for Actors
Uptown: Character Monologues for Actors
Monologues from Contemporary Literature: Volume I
Monologues from Classic Plays

## FESTIVAL MONOLOGUE SERIES
The Great Monologues from the Humana Festival
The Great Monologues from the EST Marathon
The Great Monologues from the Mark Taper Forum
The Great Monologues from the Women's Project

## YOUNG ACTORS SERIES
Great Scenes and Monologues for Children
New Plays from A.C.T.'s Young Conservatory
Great Scenes for Young Actors from the Stage
Great Monologues for Young Actors
Multicultural Monologues for Young Actors
Multicultural Scenes for Young Actors
Villeggiature: The Trilogy Condensed, Goldoni, tr. by Robert Cornthwaite

## SCENE STUDY SERIES
Scenes From Classic Plays 468 B.C. to 1960 A.D.
The Best Stage Scenes of 1993
The Best Stage Scenes of 1992
The Best Stage Scenes for Women from the 1980's
The Best Stage Scenes for Men from the 1980's

## CONTEMPORARY PLAYWRIGHTS
Romulus Linney: 17 Short Plays
Eric Overmyer: Collected Plays
Lanford Wilson: 21 Short Plays
William Mastrosimone: Collected Plays
Horton Foote: 4 New Plays
Terrence McNally: 15 Short Plays
Women Playwrights: The Best Plays of 1992
Women Playwrights: The Best Plays of 1993
Humana Festival '93: The Complete Plays
Humana Festival '94: The Complete Plays

## GREAT TRANSLATION FOR ACTORS SERIES
The Wood Demon: Anton Chekhov *translated by N. Saunders & F. Dwyer*
The Seagull: Anton Chekhov *translated by N. Saunders & F. Dwyer*
Three Sisters: Anton Chekhov *translated by Lanford Wilson*
Mercadet: Honoré de Balzac *translated by Robert Cornthwaite*

## CAREER DEVELOPMENT BOOKS
The Actor's Chekhov
Kiss and Tell: Restoration Scenes, Monologues, & History
Cold Readings: Some Do's and Don'ts for Actors at Auditions
A Shakespearean Actor Prepares
Auditioning For Musical Theater
The Camera Smart Actor

If you require pre-publication information about upcoming Smith and Kraus books, you may receive our semi-annual catalogue, free of charge, by sending your name and address to *Smith and Kraus Catalogue, P.O. Box 127 One Main Street, Lyme, NH 03768 phone 1-800-895-4331, fax 1-603-795-4427.*

# Anne Bogart
## VIEWPOINTS

edited by Michael Bigelow Dixon and Joel A. Smith

*Career Development Series*

SK
A Smith and Kraus Book

A Smith and Kraus Book
Published by Smith and Kraus, Inc.

Cover Design by Julia Hill
Cover Photograph by John Nation
Text Design by Julia Hill & Joel A. Smith
Manufactured in the United States of America

First Edition: January 1995
5 6 7 8 9 10

**Library of Congress Cataloging-in-Publication Data**

Anne Bogart: viewpoints / edited by Michael Dixon and Joel A. Smith.
—1st ed.
      p. cm. --(Career development series)
      ISBN 1-880399-80-6. --ISBN 1-880399-94-6
      1. Bogart, Anne--Criticism and interpretation. I. Dixon, Michael Bigelow. II. Smith, Joel A. III. Series.

      PN2287.B478    1995
      792'.0233'092--dc20            94-46467
                                        CIP

Smith and Kraus, Inc.
PO Box 127, 1 Main Street, Lyme, NH 03768
800-895-4331, FAX: 603-795-4427

# Acknowledgements

Jennifer Dana, Producing Director
*Saratoga International Theater Institute*

ACTORS THEATRE OF LOUISVILLE:

Margaret S. Costello
Emily Gnadinger
Jennifer Hubbard
Jeffry Blake Johnson
Jon Jory
Jennifer McMaster
Tom Nelis
Jeffrey S. Rodgers
Marilee Hebert-Slater
James Seacat
Alexander Speer
Michele Volansky
J. Christopher Wineman

*Special Thanks*
Brown-Forman Corporation

# Contents

# Photographs

# Anne Bogart
## VIEWPOINTS

# ◆ FOREWORD ◆

by Jon Jory

JON JORY IS THE PRODUCING DIRECTOR OF ACTORS THEATRE of Louisville. In 1995 he celebrated his 26th season at Actors, during which he had directed over 90 plays and produced over 600 productions for ATL. Mr. Jory has devoted his energy to the rebirth of the regional repertory and excellence in all facets of production, but especially to the encouragement of new writers and the production of new American plays. He has been responsible for developing the internationally lauded Humana Festival of New American Plays, the SHORTS Festival, the Classics in Context Festival and most recently, the Flying Solo & Friends Festival.

I walked into a rehearsal room to watch Anne Bogart work and felt very much like Alice did when she fell down the rabbit hole. It was a world where a very different logic pertained and that logic was infinitely, quintessentially theatrical. It was tantalizing and unexplainable in the same moment. There was firm directorial guidance and no guidance simultaneously. There was an agreed upon vocabulary that was at first impenetrable and yet seemed simple. The work being essayed in the room conformed immediately to my idea of good process: the more they worked, the better it got. The principles of the work produced excellent results quite quickly but they were not the principles with which Stanislavski and Brecht had hammered us into shape for decades. What on earth was going on here? I stayed.

In a culture where the best acting is done from the neck up, Anne's work is an obvious antidote. In a theatre where we've wrung every drop from Naturalism, Anne's work takes us into new territory. Objects and furniture find new use, space becomes a character, and cliché a methodology for revelation. It's rife with visual composition. It's dance done by actors in the service of dramaturgy. It's funny and tragic at the same time, like O'Casey done by gymnasts. It reclaims the theatre from the media. It's perfectly positioned to create a dialectic with current theory without everyone getting furious and going home with the ball.

Actors love Anne Bogart, even the most suspicious and hidebound. She puts them back in charge of their own process and instantly defines them as collaborators. They find themselves more creative, less frightened and still served well by the traditional craft they had honed before she came into their lives.

So here's the deal. Lots of people are going to incorporate her theory into their practice, and just like Konstantin's acolytes, many will misunderstand it, do it badly and give it a bad name. That's why, until Anne writes the book (write the book, Anne!) we're fortunate to be directly in touch with her and her company of actors so we can put our hand directly down on this sizzling batch of new ideas and intuitions at the very time they are changing and developing and thus be, as they say, directly in touch.

But until Anne writes her book, this one will have to do. And I dare you to come away without being fascinated.

◆    ◆    ◆

# ◆ THEORIES IN PRACTICE ◆

# Terror, Disorientation and Difficulty

by Anne Bogart

As a director making theatre at the cusp of the twenty-first century, I want to examine the role of certain personal aspects of the creative process, including the role of embarrassment, the role of violence, the role of stereotype, the role of humor, the role of doubt, the role of interest, and the role of cultural memory and tradition. I begin here with one of the most primal and basic human experiences: terror. What is the role of terror, of disorientation and of difficulty in my work and in the work of other theatre artists?

My first encounters with theatre were startling and exposed me to art alive with an unnamable mystery and danger. These early experiences have made it difficult for me to relate to art that is not rooted in some form of terror. The energy of individuals who face and incorporate their own terror is genuine, palpable and contagious. In combination with the artist's deep sense of play, terror makes for compelling theatre both in the creative process and in the experience of an audience.

◆

I grew up in a Navy family and we moved every year or two to a new naval base in another part of the country or another part of the world. My cultural references were Disney movies, cocktail parties, and aircraft carriers. My first brush with terror in art happened in a park in Tokyo, Japan, when I was six years old. A huge white painted face leered down at me from an immense multicolored body. I hid, terrificd, behind my mother's skirt. This horrendous and beautiful vision was my first exposure to an actor in costume wearing a mask. A few months late in the same city, I watched, terrified, as huge wooden altars borne high by drunken Japanese men charged down the streets of Tokyo on a holy day. The drunken men and the altars sporadically smashed into shop windows. The men seemed out of control, out of their minds and utterly unforgettable.

At fifteen when my father was stationed in Newport, Rhode Island, I saw my first professional theatre production at Trinity Repertory Company in Providence, Rhode Island. The National Endowment for the Humanities had granted the company enough money to bring every high school student in the state into the theatre to see their plays. I was one of those students and traveled to Providence in a big yellow school bus to see Macbeth. The production terrified, disoriented and bewildered me. I couldn't figure out my orientation to the action. The witches dropped unexpectedly out of the ceiling, the action surrounded us on big runways and I didn't understand the words. The unfamiliar spoken language was Shakespeare and the fantastic visual language, also foreign to me, was my first encounter with the poetic language of the stage where size and scale were altered. The experience was frightening but compelling. I didn't understand the play, but I knew instantly that I would spend my life in pursuit of this remarkable universe. On that day in 1967, I received my first lesson as a director: Never talk down to the audience. It was immediately clear to me that the experience of theatre was not about us understanding the meaning of the play or the significance of the staging. We were invited into a unique world, an arena that changed everything previously defined. The Trinity Company could have easily used their big grant to present facile children's theatre and fulfill their requirements to the NEH. Instead, they presented a complex, highly personal vision in a compelling, rough fashion. The production and the artists involved spoke to me directly in a visceral and fantastic manner.

Most of the truly remarkable experiences I've had in the theatre have filled me with uncertainty and disorientation. I may suddenly not recognize a building that was once familiar or I cannot tell up from down, close from far, big from little. Actors I thought that I knew are entirely unrecognizable. I often don't know if I hate or love what I am experiencing. I notice that I am sitting forward, not leaning back. These milestone productions are often long and difficult; I feel disjointed and a little out of my element. And yet I am somehow changed when the journey is completed.

◆

We are born in terror and trembling. In the face of our terror before the uncontrollable chaos of the universe, we label as much as we can with language in the hopes that once we name something we no longer fear it. This labeling enables us to feel safer but also kills the mystery in what has been labeled, removing the life and danger out of what's been defined. The artist's responsibility is to bring the potential, the mystery and terror, the trembling, back. James Baldwin wrote, "The purpose of art is to lay bare the questions which have been hidden by the answers." The artist attempts to undefine, to present the moment, the word, the gesture as new and full of uncontrolled potential.

I became a theatre director knowing unconsciously that I was going to have to use my own terror in my life as an artist. I had to learn to work in trust and not in fear of that terror. I was relieved to find that the theatre is a useful place to concentrate that energy. Out of the almost uncontrollable chaos of life, I could create a place of beauty and a sense of community. In the most terrible depths of doubt and difficulty, I have found encouragement and inspiration in my collaborations. We have been able to create an atmosphere of grace, intensity and love. I've created a refuge for myself, for actors and for audiences through the metaphor that is theatre.

I believe that theatre's function is to remind us of the big human issues, to remind us of our terror and our humanity. In our quotidian lives, we live in constant repetitions of habitual patterns. Many of us sleep through our lives. Art should offer experiences that alter these patterns, awaken what is asleep, and remind us of our original terror. Human beings first created theatre in response to the everyday terror of life. From cave drawings to ecstatic dances around numberless fires, from Hedda Gabler raising her pistol to the disintegration of Blanche Dubois, we create hopeful shapes for our distress. I have found that theatre that doesn't address terror has no energy. We create out of fear, not from a place of security and safety. According to the physicist Werner Heisenberg, artists and scientists share a common approach. They enter into their work with one hand firmly grasping the specific and the other hand on the unknown. We must trust ourselves to enter this abyss with openness, with trust in ourselves, despite the unbalance and vulnerability. How do we trust ourselves, our collaborators and our abilities enough to work within the terror we experience in the moment of entering?

William Hurt, the actor, recently interviewed in *The New York Times,* said, "Those who function out of fear, seek security, those who function out of trust, seek freedom." These two possible agendas dramatically influence the creative process. The atmosphere in the rehearsal hall, therefore, can be imbued with either fear or trust. Are the choices made in rehearsal based on a desire for security or a search for freedom? I am convinced that the most dynamic and thrilling choices are made when there is a trust in the process, in the artists and in the material. The saving grace in one's work is love, trust and a sense of humor; trust in collaborators and the creative act in rehearsal, love for the art and a sense of humor about the impossible task. These are the elements that bring grace into a rehearsal situation and onto the stage. In the face of terror, beauty is created and hence, grace.

I want to create theatre that is full of terror, beauty, love and belief in the innate human potential for change. In dreams begin responsibility. How can I begin to work with this spirit? How can I work, not to conquer, but to embrace terror, disorientation and difficulty?

◆

Every time I begin work on a new production I feel as though I am out of my league; that I know nothing and have no notion how to begin and I'm sure that someone else should be doing my job, someone assured, who knows what to do, someone who is really a professional. I feel unbalanced, uncomfortable and out of place. I feel like a sham. I usually find a way to make it through the table work on the production, where the necessary discussions, analysis and readings happen, but then always the dreaded moment arrives when it is time to put something onto the stage. How can anything be right, true or appropriate? I desperately try to imagine some excuse for doing something else, for procrastinating further. And when we do begin work on the stage, everything we set out to do feels artificial, arbitrary and affected. I'm sure that the actors think that I am out of my mind. Every time the dramaturg steps into the rehearsal hall I feel that what I am doing with the actors reflects none of our dramaturgical discussions. I feel unsophisticated and superficial. Fortunately after a stint with this dance of the absurd, I start to notice that the actors are beginning to transform the idiotic staging into something I can get enthused about and respond to.

I have spoken with a number of theatre directors and found that I am not alone in this sensation of being out of my league at the beginning of rehearsals. We all tremble before the impossibility of beginning. It is important to remember that a director's work, as with any artist, is intuitive. Many young directors make the big mistake of assuming that directing is about being in control, telling others what to do, having ideas and getting what you ask for. I do not believe that these abilities are the qualities that make a good director or exciting theatre. Directing is about feeling, about being in the room with other people—with actors, with designers, with an audience—about having a feel for time and space, about breathing and responding fully to the situation at hand, being able to plunge and encourage a plunge into the unknown at the right moment. David Salle, the painter, said in an interview, "I feel that the only thing that really matters in art and life is to go against the tidal wave of literalism and literal-mindedness to insist on and *live* the life of the imagination. A painting has to be the experience instead of pointing to it. I want to have and give *access to feeling*. That is the riskiest and only important way to connect art to the world—to make it alive. The rest is just current events."

I know that I cannot sit down when work is happening on the stage. If I sit, a deadness sets in. I direct from impulses in my body responding to the stage, the actors' bodies, their inclinations. If I sit down I lose my spontaneity, my connection to myself and to the stage, to the actors. I try to soften my eyes, that is, not to look too hard or with too much desire, because vision is dominant and eviscerates the other senses.

When I am lost in rehearsal, when I am stymied and have no idea what to do next or how to solve a problem, I know that this is the moment to make a leap. Because directing is intuitive, it involves walking with trembling into the unknown. Right there, in that moment, in that rehearsal, I have to say, "I know!" and start walking toward the stage. During the crisis of the walk, something *must* happen: some insight, some idea. The sensation of this walk to the stage, to the actors, feels like falling into a treacherous abyss. The walk creates a crisis in which innovation must happen, invention must transpire. I create the crisis in rehearsal to get out of my own way. I create despite myself and my limitations and my hesitancy. In unbalance and falling lie the potential of creation. When things start to fall apart in rehearsal, the possibility of creation exists. What we have planned before, what we have in our mind in that moment is not interesting. Rollo May wrote that all artists and scientists, when they are doing their best work, feel as though they are not doing the creating, they feel as though they are being spoken through. How do we get out of our own way in rehearsal?

The vitality, or energy, in any given work is a reflection of the artist's courageousness in the light of her own terror. For me, the essential aspect of a work is its vitality. The creation of art is not an escape from life but a penetration into it. I recently saw a retrospective of Martha Graham's early dance works. I was astonished that pieces such as *Primitive Mysteries* are now fifty years old and *still* risky and exposed. Graham once wrote to Agnes DeMille:

> There is a vitality, a life-force, a quickening that is translated through you into action, and because there is only one of you in all time, this expression is unique. And if you block it, it will never exist through any other medium and be lost. The world will not have it. It is not your business to determine how good it is; nor how valuable it is; nor how it compares with other expressions. It is your business to keep it yours clearly and directly, to keep the channel open. You do not have to believe

*in yourself or your work. You have to keep open*
*and aware directly to the urges that motivate you.*

Vitality in art is a result of articulation, energy and differentiation. All great art is differentiated art. Our awareness of the differences between things around us touches upon the source of our terror. It is more comfortable to feel similarities, yet we need to accept the terror of differences in order to create vital art. The terrible truth is that no two people are alike, no two snowflakes are alike, no two moments are alike. Physicists now say that nothing touches, nothing in the universe has contact; there is only movement and change. This is a terrifying notion given our attempt to make contact with one another. The ability to see, experience and articulate the differences between things is differentiation. Great artworks incorporate this notion of differentiation in varying ways. An exceptional painting is one which, for example, one color is highly and visibly differentiated from another, in which we see the differences in textures, shapes, spacial relationships. What made Glenn Gould a brilliant musician was his openness to high differentiation in music, which created the ecstatic intensity of his playing. In the best theatre, moments are highly differentiated. An actor's craft lies in the differentiation of one moment from the next. A great actor seems dangerous, unpredictable, full of life and differentiation.

◆

We not only need to use our terror of differentiation but also our terror of conflict. Americans are plagued with the disease of agreement. In the theatre, we often presume that collaboration means agreement. I believe that too much agreement creates productions with no vitality, no dialectic, no truth. Unreflected agreement deadens the energy in a rehearsal. I do not believe that collaboration means mechanically doing what the director dictates. Without resistance there is no fire. The Germans have a useful word that has no suitable English equivalent: *auseinandersetzung*. The word, literally "to set oneself apart from another," is usually translated into English as "argument," a word with generally negative connotations. As much as I would be happier with a congenial and easygoing environment in rehearsal, my best work emanates from *auseinandersetzung,* which means to me that to create we must set oneself apart from each other. This does not mean, "No, I don't like your approach, or your ideas." It does not mean, "No, I won't do what you are asking me to do." It means, "Yes, I will include your suggestion, but I will come at it from another angle and add these new notions." It means that we attack one another, that we may collide; it means that we may argue, doubt each other, offer alternatives. It means that I may feel foolish or unprepared. It means that rather than blindly fulfilling instructions, we examine choices in the heat of rehearsal, through repetition and trial and error. I have found that German theatre artists tend to work with too much *auseinandersetzung,* which becomes debilitating and can create static, heady productions. Americans tend towards too much agreement, which can create superficial, unexamined, facile art.

The words in this essay are easier to write than to practice in rehearsal. In moments of confrontation with terror, disorientation and difficulty, most of us want to call it a night and go home. These thoughts are meant to be reflections and notions to help give us some perspective, to help us to work with more faith and courage. I'd like to close with a quote from Brian Swimme:

> *How else can we express feelings but by entering deeply into them? How can we capture the mystery of anguish unless we become one with anguish? Shakespeare lived his life, stunned by its majesty, and in his writing attempted to seize what he felt, to capture this passion in symbolic form. Lured into the intensity of living, he represented this intensity in language. And why? Because beauty stunned him. Because the soul can not confine such feelings.*

◆    ◆    ◆

# Source-Work, the Viewpoints and Composition: What Are They?

by Tina Landau

TINA LANDAU IS A DIRECTOR AND PLAYWRIGHT. HER PLAYS
include *1969* at the Humana Festival of New American
Plays, the musical pieces *Floyd Collins* and
*States of Independence* at the American Music Theatre Festival, *American Vaudeville* with Anne Bogart at the Alley Theatre, and *In Twilite* and *Modern Fears* at American Repertory Theatre. For En Garde Arts she directed her play *Stonewall* and Charles Mee's *Orestes*. She also staged José Rivera's *Marisol* at La Jolla Playhouse.

W hen Anne's work is discussed, described, or created, certain words make their appearance over and over again: the Viewpoints. Source-work. Composition. What do these terms mean? Where did they originate? How are they used in creating work for the theatre?

BACKGROUND

I met Anne at the beginning of 1988 at the American Repertory Theater (ART) in Cambridge, Massachusetts. She had come to do a project with the acting students at the ART Institute. I had never seen Anne before, had only heard her described third-hand as "the Mama of Downtown Theatre," and had seen only half of one of her productions, having walked out during intermission, several years earlier. Out of mild curiosity, I sat in on her first rehearsal with the actors on Heinrich von Kleists's *Kätchen von Heilbronn*. Two hours later, I marched up to the head of the Institute and announced that I *had* to work with this woman. And so I became her assistant director on this project. In those two short hours, I felt the reality of what I could do, think about, and dream of in the theatre radically shift. Like many people when they first encounter Anne, I was deeply inspired by her generosity and respect for us as artists, and by the overwhelming flood of passionate, insightful theories she let loose at us that day.

Over the next three months, I worked with Anne closely on

what would be the first of our many collaborations. In our first weeks of what she called "source-work," I studied what was then called "The Six Viewpoints." I did "composition work." I ate up her methodology as someone who was starving to finally *name* the things I had always done but had no words for.

Then something scary happened. In the following year or so, as I made my own work as a writer and director, I discovered that Anne's influence had so permeated my thinking that I had somewhat lost myself. I went through a horrible period of having no idea who I was or what I wanted as an artist. It was during this time that I realized the final and most critical step I had to take in relation to Anne's methods: to make them my own. To question them. Refine them. Expand them. Find the necessity and meaning of them for myself. As is the case with all systems or sets of rules, the danger lies in a blind imitation of their form without fighting for the understanding of their essence. I remembered Anne saying that the work she did was "stolen" from a myriad of sources, most prominently the Viewpoints from a dance teacher at New York University (NYU) named Mary Overlie, and the notions of composing for the theatre from a woman named Aileen Passloff, who taught a class called "Composition" at Bard College (one of the four schools Anne attended). Over the last five years, I've struggled to develop and teach my own versions of Source-work, the Viewpoints, and Composition. Anne and I now talk about these ideas incessantly, teach classes on them together, and continue to modify them in a trading back and forth of experience and example. The following description of these methods is my understanding and use of them, inspired by Anne's understanding and use of them, in turn inspired by people like Mary Overlie's and Aileen Passloff's understanding and use of them. It is impossible to say where these ideas actually originated, for they are timeless and belong to the natural principles of movement, time and space. Over these years, we have simply articulated a set of names to put on things that already exist, that we do naturally and have always done, with greater or lesser degrees of consciousness and emphasis.

So on the one hand, I'm loathe to do what I'm about to do: Describe the nuts and bolts of an amorphous, mysterious, and to me, somewhat sacred process. My own experience taught me the dangerous seduction of trappings, of taking on a method of working or a "style" of staging. (By the way, the Viewpoints are not a style, nor do they imply a style. The Viewpoints are meant as much for naturalism as they are for postmodern abstraction.) Yet on the other hand, I know deeply the importance of structure, of guides and maps. That is what we use each time we pick up the text of a play. The text is simply the outline, the form. The form which does not become something truly alive until it is filled in with the necessity of emotion, thought, or meaning. Source-work, the Viewpoints, and Composition are also only maps. Tools and ladders. They provide a structure for the artist so she can forget about structure. They are there to free her up for the much more difficult, consuming task of expression, of getting in touch with and communicating the stuff of the soul. They exist *in the service of Art.*

## SOURCE-WORK

*Source-work* is a series of activities done at the beginning of the rehearsal process to get in touch—both intellectually and emotionally, both individually and collectively—with "the source" from which you are working.

*Source-work* is the time taken (before you begin rehearsing anything the audience is actually going to see on stage) to enter with your entire being into the world, the issues, the heart of your material.

*Source-work* can include, but is not limited to, work using the Viewpoints and Composition.

Anne believes that great theatre, whether it is a new piece you are creating or an old play you are producing, carries inside of it *a question.* It is this question, however the collaborators feel it, which is the source of their work. It is this question which needs to be discovered, awakened and brought to life for the audience. But in order for this to happen for an audience, the question must first be alive for the collaborators (not only the director or writer, but also the actors and designers). Source-work is a way of lighting the fire for everyone to share. It's not about staging. It's not about setting the final product. It is about making time at the beginning of the process—sometimes only a day or two, sometimes a month or more (depending always on time limitations)—to wake up the question inside the piece in a true, personal way for everyone involved.

A director often does Source-work on her own before rehearsals begin. Anne reads a ton of books and buys dozens of new CDs to listen to. I cut out photographs and stick them all over the walls and rent movies of a particular era or genre or subject. Other directors might go to the library, make field trips, talk to people—any kind of research or preparation which informs the work. So when a director walks into rehearsal on the first day, she is often weeks or months ahead of the rest of the company in her obsession with the material. Source-work is used to provide a similar time and space for the collaborators to fill up with their own knowledge, interest, dreams and reactions to the material. The director has caught a disease, and somehow in those critical early moments in the process she has to make the disease contagious. Source-work spreads the disease. Source-work is an invitation to obsession.

Although Anne describes the source as a question, I think of it as anything which is the origin for the work at hand. Source-work is about getting in touch with this original impulse behind the work, as well as the work itself, i.e. the text, its relevance, its period or author, or the physical and aural world of the production. The source of a theatre piece can be as intangible as a feeling or as concrete as a newspaper clipping or found object. Theatre can be made with anything as its source. Source-work is the time we put aside to "riff" off the source, to respond to it as a group, and to cause and identify an explosive chemistry between it and us.

An example of Source-work in rehearsal:

At the first rehearsal for *Kätchen von Heilbronn*, Anne asked everyone to come in on the second day with a list or presentation which answered the question "What is German?". She was interested not in academic research, which would bring us to the material from our heads, but in subjective responses which would bring us to the material from our hearts and imaginations: our preconceptions, our prejudices, our fantasies, our own memories and histories and culture. She wanted to bring our hidden selves to the surface through Source-work. So when we came in on the second day of rehearsal, one person read a list of things German, another brought in "German" food for us to eat, and I played the most clichéd "German" music I could think of on the piano, ranging from Beethoven's Fifth to the Nazi anthem "Tomorrow Belongs to Me" from *Cabaret*. In this way, we were able to identify where we were starting as a group in relationship to the play, to become aware of its context for us, and then to decide how and why to operate out of that— or not.

A second example:

When I visited Anne in rehearsal for *Strindberg Sonata* (a piece she made about Strindberg's world at the University of California at San Diego), she was in the middle of Source-work with the company. She had asked the actors to fill in the blanks: "When I think of Strindberg, I see _____, I hear _____, I smell _____," etc. On the day I visited they were reading their lists out loud. They were full of images of men in top hats and women in long gowns, crimson and black velvet, Edvard Munch paintings; the sounds of a piano playing, a clock ticking, a gun shot; the smells of paper burning, liquor on someone's breath, a bouquet of flowers...The first things that came up were often the most obvious, but Anne encouraged the actors to lean into the clichés and stereotypes rather than try to ignore them. By going through them, she explained, they would come out on the other side with something that used, but transformed them. Most importantly for me, the lists had served to waken the imaginations of the actors and to start creating the vocabulary for their "play-world."

When I direct a piece, I start with the assumption that we can create an entirely new universe on stage, a *play-world*. Rather than taking for granted that the reality of the play will be the same as our everyday reality, we instead assume that anything in this play-world can be invented from scratch. The play-world is the set of laws belonging to this piece and no other: The way time operates, the way people dress, the color palate, what constitutes good or evil, good manners or bad, what a certain gesture denotes, etc. I use Source-work to create the play-world of any given piece. Out of tasks like the one above, we develop a list which defines our new world. Sometimes these are concrete and historical (as in the way people hold cigarettes in turn-of-the century Russia so as to make them last longer), and sometimes they are invented (as in Anne's production of *Small Lives/Big Dreams* where everyone in the universe has to enter from stage right and exit stage left so that to exit stage right takes on a specific meaning of breaking the rules, leaving the game, going backwards, going towards death).

In addition to the talking and writing that we might do as a group in Source-work, it is during this time at the beginning of rehearsals that we do the Viewpoint training which subsequently leads to Composition work.

## THE VIEWPOINTS

*The Viewpoints* are a philosophy of movement translated into a technique for 1) training performers and 2) creating movement on stage.

*The Viewpoints* are the set of names given to certain basic principles of movement; these names constitute a language for talking about what happens or works on stage.

*The Viewpoints* are points of awareness that a performer or creator has while working.

Anne came into contact with the Viewpoints at NYU. When I met her, there were six Viewpoints. Today we work with nine Viewpoints, in addition to several subcategories and viewpoints which are specifically related to sound as opposed to movement. The Viewpoints overlap with each other and constantly change in relative value, depending on the artist or teacher and/or the style of the production.

*Viewpoints of Time*

▪ *Tempo*—the rate of speed at which a movement occurs; how fast or slow something happens on stage.

- *Duration*–how long a movement or sequence of movements continues; duration in terms of the Viewpoint work specifically relates to how long a group of people working together stay inside a certain section of movement before it changes.

- *Kinesthetic Response*–a spontaneous reaction to motion which occurs outside you; the timing in which you respond to the external events of movement or sound; the impulsive movement which occurs from a stimulation of the senses. An example: Someone claps in front of your eyes and you blink in response, or someone slams a door and you impulsively stand up from the chair in which you were sitting.

- *Repetition*–the repeating of something on stage. Repetition includes:
    a) Internal Repetition (repeating a movement within your own body) and
    b) External Repetition (repeating the shape, tempo, gesture, etc. of something outside your own body).

*Viewpoints of Space*

- *Shape*–the contour or outline the body (or bodies) make in space. All shape can be broken down into either:
    a) lines
    b) curves
    c) a combination of lines and curves
Therefore, in the Viewpoint training we work on creating shapes that are round, shapes that are angular and shapes that are a mixture of these two. In addition, shape can either be:
    a) stationary
    b) moving through space.
Lastly, shape can be made in one of three forms:
    a) the body in space
    b) the body in relationship to architecture making a shape
    c) the body in relationship to other bodies making a shape

- *Gesture*–a movement involving a part or parts of the body. Gestures can be made with the hands, the arms, the legs, the head, the mouth, the eyes, the feet, the stomach or any other part or combination of parts which can be isolated. Gesture is broken down into:

a) Behavioral Gesture–Behavioral Gesture belongs to the concrete, physical world of human behavior as we observe it in our everyday reality. It is the kind of gesture you see in the supermarket or on the subway. Scratching, pointing, waving, sniffing, bowing, saluting are all Behavioral Gestures. Behavioral Gesture often has a thought or intention behind it. Behavioral Gesture gives information about character, period, physical health, circumstance, weather, clothes, etc. Behavioral Gesture is usually defined by a person's character or the time and place in which they live. Behavioral Gesture can be further broken down and worked on in terms of Private Gesture and Public Gesture.

b) Expressive Gesture–Expressive Gesture expresses an inner state or emotion. It is abstract and symbolic rather than representational. It is universal and timeless and is not something you would normally see someone do in the supermarket or subway.

■ *Architecture*–the physical environment in which you are working and how awareness of it affects movement. How many times have we seen productions where there is a lavish, intricate set covering the stage and yet the actors remain down center, hardly exploring or using the surrounding architecture? In working architecture as a Viewpoint, we learn to dance with the space, to be in dialogue with a room, to let movement (especially shape and gesture) evolve out of our surroundings. Architecture is broken down into:

a) solid mass (walls, floors, ceilings, furniture, windows, doors, etc.)

b) texture (whether the solid mass is wood or metal or fabric will change the kind of movement we create in relationship to it)

c) light (the sources of light in the room, the shadows we make in relationship to these sources, etc.)

d) color (creating movement off of the colors in the space, e.g. how one red chair among many black ones would affect our choreography in relation to that chair)

In working with architecture, we create *spatial metaphors*, giving form to such feelings as I'm "up against the wall," "caught between the cracks," "trapped," "lost in space," "on the threshold," "high as a kite," etc.

▪ *Spatial Relationship*—the distance between things on stage, especially one body to another, one body to a group of bodies, or the body to the playing space. What is the full range of possible distances between things on stage? What kinds of groupings allow us to see a stage picture more clearly? Which groupings suggest an event or emotion, express a dynamic? In both real life and on the stage, we tend to position ourselves at a polite two or three foot distance from someone we are talking to. When we become aware of the expressive possibilities of Spatial Relationship on stage, we begin working with less polite but more dynamic distances of extreme proximity or extreme separation.

▪ *Topography*—the *landscape*, the *floor pattern*, or the *design* we create through movement in the space. In defining a landscape, for instance, we might decide that the downstage area has great density, is difficult to move through, while the upstage area has less density and therefore involves more fluidity and faster tempos. In working on floor pattern, we can use the image that the bottom of our feet have red paint on them and that, as we move through the space, the picture that evolves on the floor is the floor pattern which emerges to the onlooker's eye over time. The design involves choices about the size and shape of the space that is available for us to work in; for example, we might choose to work in a narrow three-foot strip all the way downstage or in a giant triangular shape which covers the whole floor, etc.

USE OF THE VIEWPOINTS IN REHEARSAL

There are as many different ways to work on the Viewpoints in rehearsal as there are rehearsal approaches. Usually, Anne will do anywhere from a day to a week of *Viewpoint Training*. As training, the Viewpoints function much as scales do for a pianist or working at the barre does for the ballet dancer. It is a structure for practice, for keeping specific "muscles" in shape, alert, flexible. The actor, in the case of the Viewpoints, exercises awareness (awareness of the different Viewpoints), the ability to listen with the entire body, and a sense of spontaneity and extremity. The actor trains to take in and use everything that occurs around her, and to not exclude anything because she thinks she knows what is good or bad, useful or not. The Viewpoints enable performers to find possibility larger than what they first imagine—whether it is in creating a shape they didn't know their body was capable of or in discovering a range of unexpected gestures for a character. By using the Viewpoints fully, we eliminate the actor's ability to state "my character would never do that." By using the Viewpoints fully, we give up our own heady decisions and judgments. By using the Viewpoints fully, we give ourselves surprise, contradiction and unpredictability.

The Viewpoints are practiced each day in rehearsal, at first separately and, after some time, together. Each rehearsal might begin with a twenty-minute Viewpoint session in which the actors will work together in an "improvisatory" fashion. The only set structure is the notion of the Viewpoints. When the SITI company rehearses, their beginning twenty-minute set each day includes working off of music and light as well. For instance, they apply the notion of Kinesthetic Response to changes in sound, so that when the sound designer Darron West suddenly changes the music, the actors immediately incorporate a response in movement. When working with music in the Viewpoints, we ask, "How can one be open to and affected by the music, without being dictated or limited by it?"

In preparing for specific work on the play, the Viewpoints can also be used to create more specific "improvisations" based on *themes*. For instance, in beginning work on *The Medium*, Anne might give the company the theme of "The Future." Using their awareness of the Viewpoints, the company will create spontaneous movement which is somehow of "The Future." Just as when we work with music, the use of a theme is intended to inspire rather than determine movement, to open up rather than limit choices. The company makes movement which is somehow expressive of "The Future" without being literal. The company then observes what patterns emerged in their Viewpoints, discusses them, and determines whether or not to include them in the vocabulary for the production. For instance, working with the theme of "The Future," the company might discover that their shapes were predominantly angular and geometric. Or that there were extreme switches of tempo from slow motion to hyperspeed. Or that the gesture of covering the eyes kept coming up. Or that they were moving on the floor pattern of a grid. These patterns can then be used as guides in staging. Or not. The director, like the actors, has worked with an *awareness* of the Viewpoints so as to create a conscious and extreme range of choice.

Anne often uses the Viewpoints as the basis for staging a piece. By using them, the actors become the individual and collective choreographers of the physical action. First, the Viewpoints are a common language that the company shares. They become a shorthand for communication. Anne can look at the stage, notice that the spacing is cluttered, say to the actors "Spatial Relationship," and they will adjust accordingly to create a more "readable" stage picture. Second, the Viewpoints are a tool for the actors to make their own staging rather than have the director tell them where to go and what to do. The information which causes movement doesn't come from a direction as much as a response to what is already happening around them in the playing space. In this way, the movement is organic and belongs to the actor. Lastly, the Viewpoints are often used to generate and then "set" the staging. Anne might ask two actors to make a movement sequence using the Viewpoints which expresses the relationship between these two characters. The text will then be "put on" the movement. In this way, Anne chooses to set the form but allow the emotional life of the characters to remain open. The staging becomes the vessel for what goes on in the interior life. Additionally, the piece begins operating on multiple "tracks" (as in film there is a visual–track and a sound-track or in music there is four- or eight- or twelve-track recording). The movement has been freed from the text so that each is informed by and related to the other without it being the same as the other. There is a tension between what is seen and what is heard, and now the spoken text allows us to see the physical text more clearly and the physical text allows us to hear the spoken text more clearly. The various "tracks" of a theatre piece can be separated, played in counterpoint, or sync-ed up to create different expressions of harmony and discord, balance and disorientation. These are only some of the ways the Viewpoints are used in moving from training to production. The Viewpoint of Gesture can be used to work on developing character. The Viewpoint of Architecture can be used to stage an entire scene around and in and on a doorway or, as Anne would say, "to make door art." The possibilities are infinite.

Finally, Anne and I have recently started doing in-depth experimentation with the Viewpoints as they relate to sound. In our classes in New York, we are currently working on applying the notions of Shape, Tempo, Gesture, Architecture, Repetition, Duration, and Kinesthetic Response to sound (abstract) and speech (sound with denotation and connotation). While the Viewpoints of Topography and Spatial Relationship have become less useful in this area, two new Viewpoints have inserted themselves into our training here: Dynamic (or volume) and Pitch (or tone). In exploring this new territory, we hope to eventually put the *Physical and Aural Viewpoints* together so that the Viewpoint sessions will include both movement and text.

COMPOSITION

*Composition* is the practice of selecting and arranging the separate components of theatrical language into a cohesive work of art for the stage. It is the same technique that any choreographer, painter, writer, composer, or filmmaker uses in their corresponding disciplines.

*Composition* is to the creator (whether director, writer, performer, designer, etc.) what the Viewpoints are to the actor: a method for practicing her art.

*Composition* is a method for revealing to ourselves our hidden thoughts and feelings about the material. Because we usually make Compositions in rehearsal in an unbelievably short amount of time (anywhere from three minutes to half an hour), we have no time to think. Composition provides a structure for working from our impulses and intuition.

*Composition* is a method for generating, defining and developing the theatre vocabulary that will be used for any given piece. In Composition, we make pieces so that we can point to them and say, "That worked," and ask, "Why?"—so that we can then articulate which ideas, moments, images, etc., we will include in our production.

*Composition* is a method for creating new work. It is an alternative method of writing. Rather than being alone in a room with a computer, Composition is writing with a group of people on their feet. In creating the drug trips for my piece *1969* at last year's Humana Festival of New American Plays or in Anne's creating her Brecht piece *No Plays No Poetry*, we both employed the magic of Composition to have the company generate tons of material which we then sifted through as a film editor would, selecting which material to use and in what order.

*Compositions* are assignments we give to the company to have them create short, specific theatre pieces addressing a particular aspect of the work. Anne and I use Composition during the Source-work period of a rehearsal to engage the collaborators in the process of generating their own work around the source. The assignment will usually include an overall intention or structure as well as a substantial list of ingredients which must be included in the piece. This list is the raw material of the theatre language we'll speak in the piece—whether principles that are useful for staging (symmetry versus asymmetry, use of scale and perspective, juxtaposition, etc.) or the ingredients that belong specifically to the play-world we are working on (these can be objects, textures, colors, sounds, actions, etc.). These ingredients are to a Composition what single words are to a paragraph or essay. The creator makes meaning by their arrangement. In addition, in Composition work we study and use principles from other disciplines as translated to the stage. For example, stealing from music, we might ask what the rhythm of a moment is, or how to interact based on a fugue structure, or how a coda functions and whether or not we should add one...Or we'll think about film and ask, "How do we stage a close-up (i.e. what is its equivalent in the theatre?). An establishing shot? A montage?" In applying compositional principles from other disciplines to the theatre, we push the envelope of theatrical possibility and challenge ourselves to create new forms.

◆

The following is an imaginary, but typical Composition assignment that Anne or I might give to actors in the first week of rehearsal for a Chekhov play or a piece about Chekhov:

Divide into groups of five. Each group will create a 6 minute piece which is an expression of a "Chekhovian" world.

The piece should be in three parts, each with a clear beginning and end, and each separated by a device (a blackout, a voice-over, a bell, etc.). The three parts are titled:
1) The way things look in this world
2) The way things sound in this world
3) The way people are in this world

*You* must *include in your Composition piece:*

■ All the Viewpoints.

■ A setting (somewhere in this building) which is the perfect architectural environment for your piece.

- A clear role for the audience (Are we voyeurs? Judges? Historical archeologists? Etc.).

- A Revelation of Space (for example, the curtain rises and we see the stage, or a door opens and we see endless corridors behind it).

- A Revelation of Object (for example, someone opens a box and there is a gun inside it).

- A Surprise Entrance.

- Music from an Unexpected Source (for example, the doctor opens his medical bag and the aria of an operatic soprano emanates from inside it).

- 15 Seconds of Simultaneous Unison Action.

- Broken Expectation.

- A Staged Accident.

- Two Uses of Extreme Contrast (loud/quiet, fast/slow, dark/bright, violent/gentle, still/chaotic, etc.).

- The Objects:
  A gun
  A cigarette
  Playing cards
  A tea cup
  Fire in any form

- The Sounds:
  A clock chiming
  Birds chirping
  Someone singing offstage
  Silverware clinking

- The Actions:
  Tripping over something
  An embrace
  A slap
  Whispering
  "Laughing through tears"

- The only text you can use is:
  I was so happy.
  Do you remember?
  Whatever do you think has come over her (him) today?
  Two hundred years from now, I wonder if human kind will
    still be suffering?
  My boot.
  Do you hear the wind?
  We must go on living.
  We must work.

  *You have twenty minutes to make your piece. Go.*

◆

And *that* is the joy of Composition work. And that is also the
beautiful, large, courageous spirit with which Anne works.

◆　◆　◆

# Directorial Credits

# A Production History

## 1995

*The Adding Machine* by Elmer Rice, Actors Theatre of
   Louisville: Louisville, KY
*The Medium* created by the SITI Company, Actors Theatre of
   Louisville: Louisville, KY
*Small Lives/Big Dreams* created by the SITI Company, Actors
   Theatre of Louisville: Louisville, KY

## 1994

*Small Lives/Big Dreams* derived from the five major plays of
   Anton Chekhov, created by The Saratoga International The-
   ater Institute: Toga-mura, Japan and Saratoga Springs, NY
*The Women* by Claire Booth Luce, Hartford Stage: Hartford, CT
*Escape from Paradise* by Regina Taylor, Circle Repertory Com-
   pany: New York, NY
*Marathon Dancing* by Laura Harrington, Musical adaptation and
   supervision by Christopher Drobny, En Garde Arts: New
   York, NY
*Hot 'N' Throbbing* by Paula Vogel, American Repertory Theatre:
   Cambridge, MA

## 1993

*Marathon Dancing* by Laura Harrington, Musical adaptation and
   supervision by Christopher Drobny,workshop–Lava & En
   Garde Arts: New York, NY
*Behavior in Public Places,* Via Theatre St. Marks: New York, NY
*Hot 'N' Throbbing* by Paula Vogel, workshop–Circle Repertory
   Company: New York, NY
*The Medium* based on the life and predictions of Marshall
   McLuhan, created by The Saratoga International Theater In-
   stitute: Saratoga Springs, NY & Toga-mura, Japan

# The Medium

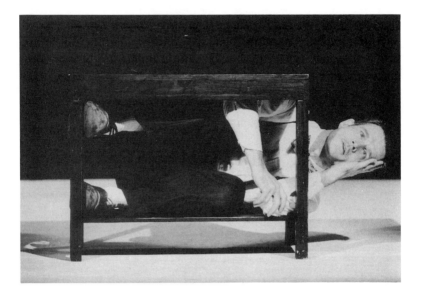

Tom Nelis in *The Medium*

*Photograph by Joan Marcus*

# 1992

*Picnic* by William Inge, Actors Theatre of Louisville: Louisville, KY

*Orestes* by Charles L. Mee, Jr., The Saratoga International Theater Institute: Saratoga Spings, NY and Toga-mura, Japan

*The Women* by Claire Boothe Luce, San Diego Repertory Theatre: San Diego, CA

*American Vaudeville* by Anne Bogart and Tina Landau, Alley Theater: Houston, TX

*The Baltimore Waltz* by Paula Vogel, Circle Repertory Company: New York, NY & The Alley Theater: Houston, TX

# 1991

*In The Jungle of Cities* by Bertolt Brecht, Mabou Mines at the Public Theater: New York, NY

*Another Person is a Foreign Country* by Charles L. Mee, Jr., En Garde Arts: New York, NY

*In The Eye of the Hurricane* by Eduardo Machado, Actors Theatre of Louisville: Louisville, KY

# 1990

*Once in a Lifetime* by Kaufman and Hart, American Repertory Theatre: Cambridge, MA

*On the Town* Music by Leonard Bernstein, Book and Lyrics by Betty Comden and Adolph Green, Based on an idea by Jerome Robbins, Trinity Repertory Company: Providence, RI

# 1989

*Summerfolk* by Maxim Gorky, Trinity Repertory Company: Providence, RI

*No Plays No Poetry* revival–Performed by members of Via Theater, The Talking Band and Otrabanda Company, Trinity Repertory Company: Providence, RI

*Life is a Dream* by Calderon de la Barca, American Repertory Theatre: Cambridge, MA

*Strindberg Sonata* written and directed by Anne Bogart and Jeff Halpern, based on the works of August Strindberg, Developed and performed at UCSD at the Mandell Weiss Center for the Performing Arts: La Jolla, CA

# Picnic

(*foreground*) Karenjune Sánchez (*background*) Victor Gonzalez,
Brooke Channon and Tracey Maloney in *Picnic*
*Photograph by Richard Trigg*

## 1988

*Once in a Lifetime* by George S. Kaufman and Moss Hart, River
Arts Repertory: Woodstock, NY

*Kätchen von Heilbronn* by Heinrich von Kleist, American
Repertory Theatre Institute: Cambridge, MA

*No Plays No Poetry* adapted from the theoretical writings of
Bertolt Brecht, Produced by Via Theater, The Talking Band
and Otrabanda Company: Ohio Theatre, NY

*Cinderella/Cendrillon* adapted from the opera *Cendrillon* by
Jules Massenet, text by Eve Kunsler, Via Theater and Music-
Theatre Group: St. Clement's Church, NY

## 1987

*Assimil* an original dance theater work produced by Via Theater
and the Danspace Project: St. Mark's Church, NY

*In His Eightieth Year* by Gillian Richards, Produced by BACA
Downtown and Cement Theater: Brooklyn, NY

*Where's Dick?* an opera by Stuart Wallace and Michael Korie,
Opera Omaha: Omaha, NE

*Cinderella in a Mirror* based on the opera *Cendrillon* by Jules
Massenet, text by Wendy Kesselman, Music-Theatre Group
at Lenox Arts Center: Stockbridge, MA

*Babel* an original work performed by the Theater Zum Westlis-
chen Stadthirschen (Berlin), produced by West Berlin's 750
year Festival in four locations in West Berlin

*The Dispute* by Pierre Marivaux, UCSD at the Mandell Weiss
Center for the Performing Arts: La Jolla, CA

## 1986

*Danton's Death* by Georg Büchner, translation by Howard Bren-
ton, NYU's Tisch School of the Arts: NY

*Cleveland* by Mac Wellman, BACA Downtown: Brooklyn, NY

*Between Wind* by Jessica Litwak, Music-Theatre Group, Lenox
Arts Center: Stockbridge, MA

*1951* by Mac Wellman and Anne Bogart, New York Theatre
Workshop: Perry Street Theatre, NY

*1951* by Mac Wellman and Anne Bogart, UCSD at the Mandell
Weiss Center for the Performing Arts: La Jolla, CA

*1951, Les Traces*, American Center: Paris, France

# Small Lives/Big Dreams

(*foreground*) J. Ed Araiza, Karenjune Sánchez,
and Kelly Maurer (*background*) Will Bond and Jefferson Mays
in *Small Lives/Big Dreams*
*Photograph by Clemens Kalischer*

# 1985

*The Making of Americans* based on the novel by Gertrude
Stein, music by Al Carmines, libretto by Leon Katz, Music-
Theatre Group: Stockbridge, MA and St. Clement's Church,
NY

*Catsman, Leo, Miranda, Stiff* (four one-act operas from *One
Aria Opera*) Texas Opera Theater: Houston, TX

*The Women* by Claire Booth Luce, Bennington College: Bennington, VT

*Albanian Softshoe* by Mac Wellman, staged reading, River Arts
Repertory: Woodstock, NY

# 1984

*Spring Awakening* by Frank Wedekind, with music by Lieber
and Stoller, NYU's Tisch School of the Arts: NY

*South Pacific* by Rodgers and Hammerstein, NYU's Tisch School
of the Arts: NY

*Inge: How They Got There* based on texts by William Inge,
co-directed with John Bernd, Performance Space 122: NY

# 1983

*History, an American Dream* an original dance theatre piece,
Danspace Project: St. Mark's Church, NY

*Grid* an original theatre piece, Werkhaus Mosach, Munich, West
German; toured to Italy, Germany, and Austria

*Sommer Nachts Traum/Lost and Found* an original dance theatre piece, Munich Theater Festival: Munich, West Germany

*At the Bottom* an adaptation of *The Lower Depths* by Maxim
Gorky, NYU's Experimental Theater Wing: NY

*Cordial Panic,* three plays by Noel Coward, performed simultaneously, University of the Street: NY

# 1982

*Women and Men, A Big Dance* an original dance theatre piece,
Performance Space 122: NY

*The Ground Floor and Other Stories* an original theatre piece,
University of the Street: NY

*Small Town/Big Dreams* an original dance theatre piece, Dance
Gallery: Northampton, MA

# In the Eye
## of the Hurricane

(*L to R*) Pamela Stewart, Suzanne Costallos,
Christopher McCann, Diane D'Aquila and Bob Burrus in
*In the Eye of the Hurricane*
*Photograph by Richard Trigg*

*Sehnsucht* an adaptation of *A Streetcar Named Desire* by Tennessee Williams, Abia Theatre: Northampton, MA
*Die Gier Nach Banalem* an original theatre work, Theatre am Montag: Bern, Switzerland
*Between the Delicate* an original theatre work, Theatre am Montag: Bern, Switzerland

## 1981

*Leb Oder Tot* an original theatre work, Hochschule der Kunste: Berlin, West Germany
*I'm Starting Over, I'm Starting Over Again* an original theatre work, August Moon Arts Festival: Catskill, NY
*Exposed!* an original theatre work based on the works of Alfred Hitchcock, NYU's Experimental Theater Wing: NY
*Dance on the Volcano* an original theatre work, NYU's Experimental TheaterWing: NY

## 1980

*The Emissions Project* an original conception involving a new piece each week performed as a soap opera in different locations: NY
*Artourist* an original dance theatre work, co-directed with Mary Overlie, NYU's Experimental Theater Wing: NY
*Out of Sync* an adaptation of Anton Chekhov's *The Seagull,* self-produced: NY

## 1979

*Haupstadt* an original theatre work, NYU's Experimental Theater Wing: NY

## 1978

*Inhabitat* an original theatre work self-produced: New York City

## 1977

*RD1, The Waves* an adaptation of Virginia Wolfe's *The Waves,* co-produced by Theatre for the New City and The Iowa Theater Lab, performed in New York, California, Wisconsin, Pennsylvania and Canada

# Cinderella/Cendrillon

Joan Elizabeth and Lauren Flanigan in
*Cinderella/Cendrillon*
*Photograph by Jennifer Kotter*

## 1976

*Two Portraits* by DeeDee O'Connel, New York and San Francisco

*Macbeth* an adaptation of Shakespeare's play: The Brook, NY

# Award and Honors

1991–1993 President of Theatre Communications Group

1990 OBIE Award—Best Direction for *The Baltimore Waltz*

1988 OBIE Award—Best Direction for *No Plays No Poetry But Philosophical Reflections Practical Instructions Provocative Prescriptions Opinions and Pointers From a Noted Critic and Playwright*

1986-87 Recipient of a National Endowment for the Arts Artistic Associate Grant in association with Music-Theatre Group

1984 BESSIE Award (New York Dance and Performance) Choreographer/Creator Award for *South Pacific*

1980 Villager Award (Presented by the New York newspaper, *The Villager*)—Best Direction for *Out of Sync*

# ◆ COLLABORATORS' VIEWS ◆

# Imaging Anne:
# A Dramaturg's Notebook
by Gregory Gunter

GREGORY GUNTER IS LITERARY MANAGER/DRAMATURG FOR The New York Theatre Workshop. He's also Company Dramaturg with SITI and has worked with Anne Bogart on the SITI productions *Orestes, The Medium* and *Small Lives/Big Dreams.*

I've been fortunate to work as dramaturg and imagist with Anne on a number of projects. We met while I was dramaturging Tina Landau's production of Charles L. Mee, Jr.'s *Orestes* at the American Repertory Theatre Institute. Tina had asked me to find some images for the play so I spent about four days scouring the recesses of the Harvard libraries for books of photographs which related to it. I literally covered a thirty-five foot section of wall with a collage of pictures using an occupational therapy technique I learned during my unfortunate incarceration in a loony bin in Texas. I had used techniques of story-boarding a play via visual stimuli as an actor and playwright which I also incorporated into the mural.

This visual interpretation of the text, if you will, told the story of the House of Atreus from all points in history. Scenes from the girlhood of Clytemnestra and Helen of Troy were juxtaposed with broken Greek statues representing the death of Agamemnon. I also attempted to find a lighter side of some of the tragic family members. For instance, "Menelaus' hairy backside" was enlarged from a picture of a wealthy older man in a very small and unflattering bathing suit. The idea, then, was to create a past, present and future for each of the characters, with each relationship and each major action explored through images. The images were photocopies, of course, used for educational purposes only and were not to be displayed except in rehearsal to protect against copyright infringement. They provided the actors access into the characters in a way that hadn't before seemed possible.

◆

Anne, having seen this visual imagery project, asked to use it in Japan. So I gathered all of the images and created a book in the same style as the wall display. Her own production of *Orestes* would inaugurate her new theatre company, the Saratoga International Theatre Institute, which she formed with Tadashi Suzuki. It rehearsed in Toga, Japan. Her production would be radically different from Tina's but could still use the "historical material" provided by my research. Actors in Toga were invited to look at the book at the beginning of rehearsal and were encouraged to peruse it throughout. Anne had the actors utilize certain poses of the real-life characters in the photographs as a way of entering a "state" on the stage. Ellen Lauren, who was acting in Suzuki's *Bacchae* at the time, told me the actors treated it as a bible for the production and that the images allowed them access to a world they could not find in the mountains of Toga. Soon after Anne asked me to work on another play she was developing based on the life and writings of Marshall McLuhan.

At a meeting regarding this new play, Anne presented me a list of things she knows and doesn't know about the piece. The "Things I know" list for *The Medium* included (although this is from my recollection and not an actual list): The play is about Marshall McLuhan; McLuhan is one of the characters in the play; all the other characters are dead or part of his memory; the play takes place during the moment of his stroke, etc. From this list I compiled a list of images to locate. From the first point, "The play is about Marshall McLuhan," I asked myself some of the same questions that Anne asked: "Who is McLuhan?" "What does he look like?" "What was his home life like?" etc. So I found images of McLuhan, his family, his workplaces, his hometown. The second point only made the need for physical images of McLuhan stronger—and though Tom Nelis, who was playing McLuhan, created his own unique character, the images at least provided the company with some of the physical states of the man. The third point from the above list, "all of the other characters are dead..." led me to images of death, memory, and images of people who appear "dead" even though they're walking, interacting, etc. Some of these images were of people who'd undergone strokes. It's important for Anne, I've found, to follow every impulse—that's part of what keeps her work so vital and alive. I never knew until she or her company of actors really delved into the material what would strike them, but following intuition and my growing knowledge of Anne's needs as a director, I found things that enabled them to get a handle on a scene or a character.

The "Things I don't know" list was more complex, because I knew she'd discover those points of confusion while working with the actors. This list included: Is Marshall McLuhan the only one who's had a stroke? What physical manifestations of stroke do the other characters have? Are the other characters dead all the time? What is the world of the other characters when they're not in "television land?" From this list I began to get ideas about what Anne was searching for. The first question was hard for me to work with so I moved on to the next and found examples of physical manifestations of strokes. I went to the Aphasia Institute, interviewed a doctor there and found information on stroke victims, such as what specifically happens to them during the stroke and after. I searched for other avenues which might lead me to answers for the cast. I called stroke networks for material and dropped by the American Heart Association for pamphlets. The third question "Are all the other characters dead all the time?" was answered by the next. They, like McLuhan, were hurled into this techno world of pop philosophy primarily through McLuhan's exploration of television. They became characters. Because Anne never watched television as a child and had no references for the sit-coms, westerns and detective stories she wanted to use to tell the story, I found images of "television land." And finally, for the question "When they're not in television land where are they?" I looked at the blank screen of my own television and imagination. I found images of broken sets, blank sets, blurry screens, "snow". The actors constructed from these images the place of the characters in between scenes.

As imagist, I usually riff on an idea until it's completely spent. So images of memory, a hard thing to find, let me tell you, could be classic Americana, "the good old days," a copy of *Mc-Calls* from the 1960s, or obvious images such as a picture of a man who appears to be thinking juxtaposed with an image of a young woman holding her fingers to her chin as if perplexed. I use an active imagination to find connections and dichotomies where perhaps they didn't exist before. I try to ask myself what I would need as an actor or what would excite me about this research. Anne uses the work to stimulate her actors to stretch their imaginations beyond literal exploration. She asks a lot of her actors. She asks them to create a wholly different physical life for the play than the one most of them are comfortable using, to heighten reality to an exhausting point at times. The images then are a springboard for her company members to begin from. They move beyond it quickly, because each actor brings with her/himself a great wealth of imagination and experience. But there will always be one image to refer back to, one body position to recreate to achieve a state of being unlike any other and that's rewarding.

◆

Another rewarding aspect of dramaturging with Anne is that I'm seldom in the place that she's working. Often I don't get to see the finished product. So, while Anne was working on *The Medium* in Japan, she called saying, "We need inventions of the future." I scoured used bookstores for some far-out philosopher's book on the new teleworld. I read *Omni* and *Futurist* for predictions of things to come both phantasmagoric and economy-related. And I faxed. I didn't actually see any part of the play until I saw the video of the actors' presentation at Saratoga Springs the following September. Later, New York Theatre Workshop (NYTW) produced the play so I was able to fully experience the collaborative way in which Anne works, but I didn't feel less involved because I was far away. Anne would contact me through fax or through message saying how important the work was to them, how grateful they were for the research and ideas I was sending their way. She told me later that she and the actors sat around a large table in the rehearsal hall hungrily devouring each missive, discussing it and relating it to the work at hand.

Prior to *The Medium's* production at NYTW, I created pre-production imagery for Anne's production of *The Women* at Hartford Stage Company. She told me little about her ideas initially because, she said, they weren't fully formed. She said she wanted to get into the world of Clare Booth Luce and play with Clare's idea of angry women—how women betray each other and how much more bitter they feel when stung by a girlfriend than a man. She also knew that it would probably be set in the thirties.

So for six or seven months, I began collecting images of "angry women." I also read feminist tracts as well as interviews of politicized and marginalized women. I found old 1800s photos of women with muskets, bull dykes with raised fists, and women fighting. I also tracked down every image of Clare Booth Luce I could find. Her world, her society friends, her family, images of her as ambassador all came in to play. Now, from this collection of a hundred or so, I ultimately chose fifty or sixty for the Visual Interpretation, but I had a wide range from which to choose. When I put the piece together, I also found wonderful Art Deco poses of women-shaped vases or lamps. Pictures of women from the fashions of the thirties—which I included for the designer as well whether she or he used them or not—also became part of the fabric of the piece because it showed how stylish women of the period appeared.

During rehearsal in Hartford, Anne had the visual imagery displayed in the room. The whole piece was approximately thirty feet long by six feet wide so there were hundreds of images to take in. The actors were encouraged to look at it, to find poses from the period pictures and to explore the "character" that was Luce. When I went to see the play, I could see evidence of the work in everything from the precise turn of the ankle by Ellen Lauren (which resembled one of the fashion pictures) or the gymnastic stretch by Karenjune Sánchez (which consciously or unconsciously modeled the Art Deco pose of a woman-shaped figurine). The images fed into this production on an obvious level, the pictures were in the movement of the actors. Anne had utilized mannerisms of the period, attitudes of women vis-à-vis facial expression and stance—using the visual research.

Anne asked me to create a similar project for her production of Paula Vogel's *Hot 'N' Throbbing* at the American Repertory Theatre. Jill Robbins, a close friend, was production dramaturg, so I tried to coordinate my preproduction imagery with the work she was doing. Anne particularly wanted hard-core pornography for the visual layout. The world of pornography so accessible on 42nd Street where NYTW's offices are located is quite removed from the few places in Boston where such material is available. So I was free to play, as it were.

*Hot 'N' Throbbing* is about a woman who writes erotic stories to support herself. She's escaped from an abusive, sex-obsessed man, into economic security via the porn industry. (Forgive this oversimplification of Ms. Vogel's intriguing play.) I found anonymous porn text from book vendors on Eighth Street and incorporated it into the design of the visual imagery. I also took both pro and con articles from various feminist and fine art publications to balance out numerous pictures of large breasted go-go dancers, dominatrices in leather standing over roped-up naked males, bound women and ads for phone sex. I also scoured the book shops on 42nd Street (and the street itself) for flyers of a sexual nature to add to the imagery—to give it a little realism, I suppose. Because of the wealth of pornographic renderings available, I actually toned down the hard–core aspects (although some of the people in rehearsal might tell you otherwise) and concentrated instead on pictures which told stories of dominance and obsession which Anne stressed in her interpretation of the play.

◆

In April of 1994, when NYTW presented *The Medium*, I was able to work closely with Anne and the SITI company and for the first time see the work as it developed. There were changes that needed to take place in the play. Anne wanted it to grow; there were weak spots which needed rewriting. She asked the company members, crew and me to bring in new material for several sections. We sat on stage at various times while Anne read new text ideas, things she'd culled from her own reading since the play was first produced the previous fall. She led the actors through the Seven Viewpoints work each day; first each Viewpoint specifically, then allowing them to explore each simultaneously. Almost every day during the early part of rehearsal, she found something in the Viewpoints to incorporate into the piece. Later, even after the play was running, Anne watched the actors warming up with the Viewpoints. She was using it as a starting point for a companion piece that the company would put together in Toga.

"*The Medium*," in Anne's words, "explores what the future means to us. Now, I want to explore the past." She began telling me what she knew about her next play, *Small Lives/Big Dreams*. She knew the piece was based on the writing of Chekhov. She knew that it was going to actually be taken from Chekhov—reformed and re-created into an exploration of memory. She knew that it began after a cataclysmic event that caused a kind of global amnesia in the characters of the play.

Again, I began collecting images of memory, but this time damaged, interrupted, distorted memory. Some images were taken from blurry filmstrip, some were taken from screwed up faces of amateur models or out-of-focus photographs. Anne also wanted images of people in shock...so I faxed image after image to Japan, then followed it up with the book. She wanted text on memory, so I researched scholarly texts on memory and memory recall as well as personal accounts of Alzheimer patients, amnesia patients, and people whose memories were displaced because of trauma or shock.

As I was reading book after book about trauma related memory loss, I began to think it would be helpful to Anne if I shared my own difficulties with memory. I am a survivor of child sexual abuse, and as such, a large part of my childhood memories were repressed or displaced—my memory at present is sometimes affected by a variety of stresses which I believe stem from these early traumatic incidents. I have also experienced a variety of "flashbacks" (resurfacing memories) of the abuse. I wanted to relate to the cast the physical manifestations of these memories so that they could use them in exploring memory loss and return. At the risk of being considered self-indulgent, I faxed the company in Toga a detailed account of my experiences of memory loss and recall. I tried to explain the tangible nuances of one type of flashback over another which manifest themselves in facial and corporeal gestures. Anne faxed me back quite sincerely later and told me that she had been stumbling over the last section of the piece for days. When she received my fax, she was able to use it to determine the final movement of *Small Lives/Big Dreams.*

◆

When I dramaturg for Anne Bogart I try to think of myself as a member of the ensemble. I know that she considers every idea from every person in the room, from actor to production assistant, as part of the whole process of discovery. When I am working on a visual imagery project, somewhere miles away from where the actual rehearsal will occur (which is usually the case), I first immerse myself in the play. Then, much as Anne does before a production, I ask myself hundreds of questions. I think about each character's past, present and future; each relationship no matter how trivial is represented and explored in my work—particularly as imagist for the play. I know that Anne's sense of heightened reality (pardon that boorish term) produces connections where a conventional director might find none. Through Anne's techniques of questioning each moment, of collaborating with each participant, and of exploring the life of the play through the Seven Viewpoints, my work is going to have an impact on the style of the piece, or the movement of the actors, or the life of the play.

◆　◆　◆

# Seven Points of View

by Ellen Lauren

ELLEN LAUREN IS A COMPANY MEMBER OF THE SARATOGA
International Theater Institute and has worked ex-
tensively with both Anne Bogart and Tadashi Suzuki.
Ms. Lauren's acting credits include her performance
as Madge in the 1993 Actors Theatre of Louisville
production of *Picnic,* directed by Anne Bogart.

# 1.

I have seen the director Anne Bogart turn redder than any human really ought to be able to survive. I've also seen her drop a fairly agile Frenchman to his knees with what can only be described as a "death grip." The former takes place every few hours in the course of a rehearsal due to anger, excitement, moral crisis or rude sound. The latter took place in a kitchen in the remote mountains of western Japan. It was a mysterious thing, this laying-on of hands, that barely seemed to touch the fellow. He hit the floor with a yelp and was released only when they were both consumed with giggles. She can do that, you know. Touch something ever so slightly with a thought, a suggestion and the situation will burst into urgent activity. She can stand for hours propped up against a hard metal stool, a music stand nearby holding a script. If you should come close and peek at that script, what you would often find instead are scattered quotes, an indecipherable numerical system, labeling bits of text, lifted dialogue, a musical reference or indeed—blank space. Anne can look down at that blank space and with that deft but powerful touch sculpt it into an expression of the neurotic, aching times in which we live—push it violently, with the lightest tap, into a reflection of the group of actors before her.

I have been asked to write about Anne and somewhere between my enthusiastic acceptance and now, the prospect took on enormous weight. I feel very sure what riveted me about Anne from the start, but I am painfully aware how, once set down, words can deceive. Anne defies categories and descriptions, and surely the reader, like myself, is just as averse to reading about that which cannot be explained through anything but the work itself.

I look out my airplane window. I'm somewhere roughly over St. Petersburg on my way to Vienna from Tokyo. I think about the task ahead and all this man I'm working with, Tadashi Suzuki, has taught me. He introduced Anne and myself. Suddenly, finally, the words come easily. The blushing and the event of bringing that particular Frenchman down are impressive. And I could tell you more. But what really impressed me is the fact that Anne Bogart is engaged in preserving and deepening the single critical relationship in the theatre, that between the audience and the actor. That relationship depends on one thing only: the thrill of the fiction. It is contingent on how any one moment unfolds, and the depth to which the audience can believe in it. This is the art of acting.

It is what Anne, even despite herself sometimes, focuses on. It is why actors flock to her hungrily and leave feeling renewed. I can't write about directing. I don't believe that's what, essentially, the theatrical experience is. It's about how an idea is communicated as complexly, succinctly, thoroughly and originally as possible. That rests in the body and spirit of the actor. I am interested in what Anne is doing toward the reinstated status of the American actor. I'm sometimes not even sure if she understands this. Listen to me, Anne. I've been asked to write about you. Much is written. I've been interviewed for five different dissertations on you, asking about your humanity, that big profound life force you have. But reading about these things isn't going to do you any good. Listen. I think you're doing the right thing. Pay attention. Never less. Could be more.

Anne lets you say things like that to her. She'll listen and attack, crab-like, the issue from a wholly different angle.

# 2.

The director Anne Bogart and I met for the first time in the summer of 1986. I don't remember it at all. She came to Togamura, Japan with Peter Zeisler and Mark Lamos as a guest of Tadashi Suzuki. Mr. Suzuki and his remarkable company have turned a small farming village in the mountains into an artists colony that hosts an international arts festival every year. I remember Mark and Peter quite clearly from the kitchen duty I served and passing in dormitory hallways. Mark was funny, amiable, healthy. He'd expertly remove the yolk from his morning egg. It was always an event on any occasion Peter came over, being a longtime champion of the Suzuki Company of Toga (SCOT), but that summer I remember particularly because he got a private phone installed in his tatami room. Living communally through the long summer, these are the issues that impress. But I don't remember Anne.

You'd think I would. The signature wild pyramid of hair and battered Mary Janes were, I'm sure, the same. Her accessibility to all around her and voracious appetite for knowledge, no less than now. For whatever reasons, we did not register on each other's radar. It was not until I sat listening to the directing symposium she and Mr. Lamos conducted that I made a sighting. They both illustrated their ideas with slides of their past productions. Mark seemed more organized, relaxed, his slides lush and opulent. Then Anne spoke. Her pictures were all tight shots of actors. It's all she really addressed—the care and feeding of actors. There was a trust, even a sense of holiness as she spoke about acting—and her pictures only proved her jumbled lecture. I remember thinking, "Here's an interesting one. This one can be trained...and hooboy, look at her blush."

A few years later we met again at an opening night party in Mito, Japan. Actress Kelly Maurer and myself had been cast as guest artists in a production of Suzuki's *Dionysus*, a role that has become as constant in my life as another family member. Much had transpired between Mr. Suzuki and Ms. Bogart and we were all about to launch the first season of the Saratoga International Theater Institute (SITI) that coming summer. The plan was to rehearse and perform in Toga, then move to Saratoga Springs, New York, for more performance and training sessions. That night the summer seemed a long way off. I had just survived for the first time the agony of Agave in front of a lot of people and cameras. Anne approached me, extended her hand and said one word. It was enough. It wasn't false on her part and it was in English. The word is my secret and remains so, basically because it can only hold meaning for me on that big night so long ago.

Later that night she would tell me I was to play Electra in Chuck Mee's *Orestes* in the upcoming SITI season. I had that joyful panic rush an actor gets when their dance card is filled. Anne moved about the sparkling room speaking Greek, French and German. She seemed possessed of an inquisitiveness that I later came to recognize as a need for attention and stimulation in the deepest sense. At the same time, she remains wholly indifferent to the grubby realities of the theatre world. She has found herself repeatedly in the center of tempests, not independent of her own making, and survives with an outward restless remoteness. She is simply too busy with her own agenda to stop. It is in spite of, or because of this detachment that Anne remains sensitive to the world around her. She's a thinker and then the dreams come. She accesses knowledge then uses it on a daily basis, rolls it through her bones. She seems to let the world in like a rush of fresh air to clean, inspire, sweep away what it will. Her attentive memory puts up ideas, stories and facts like so many jars in a cupboard after summer.

She is not strictly a collector though it seemed that way to me at first. Her pragmatism and understanding of what to do with that busy mind have inspired her to develop a vocabulary for actors. When I met Anne Bogart these were called The Seven Viewpoints—though now they have expanded to just being called The Viewpoints. Anne is very clear about the variety of influences that helped her formulate this language. Influence is not a dirty word. Her appetite for influence only reflects her depth of character. She devotes her days to distilling the world into a language through which the creative process also becomes the collective process.

## 3.

I fear it's a resounding flop, this *Orestes*. We sit, Anne and I, on the steps to the studio in the morning heat. We both show up too early for rehearsals. I smoke, she sits close and breathes it in. Lights another for me. We listen to the river and talk about our lives. Like myself, raised military, Anne has no hometown. Like myself, the band of people who populate the world of whatever piece she's involved in are her neighbors. Across the backyard fence we chat. I'm finding her maddening—Mother Theresa one moment, callous the next. Just when I think that's it, she shows enormous capacity to listen. I'm struggling with this tool belt, those Seven Viewpoints she's given us. I know they function but it's as if the instructions to assemble are all in a foreign language. This body I've spent so many long years training under Mr. Suzuki's tutelage feels wooden and belligerent. My own discipline is choking me off. Now I'm scared. Mr. Suzuki is less than pleased with my performance as either Electra or Agave that summer in Toga. He's pressuring me to change my attack on Electra. Anne offers little but a quiet "Stay your course." I watch the other actors in the cast begin to speak in sentences with the grammar Anne's laid out. I see the evidence that these seven points of concentration are communication, but I can't get in. I work myself into a state, and should I have taken the mature tact, I would have seen I'm more Electra offstage than on. I'm infuriated as Anne only sits there offering up seven labels to bits of movements. She's asking me to front for her, to make sense and meaning of a theory she's developing, she says, to empower actors.

Anne is a person who makes a problem just sit there on the table like a turd. It just sits there. There's no getting around it, only a straight line drive into its source. I realize finally, painfully, the problem is none other than myself. I realize I've been trying to avoid the butt naked failing her system sets you up for. I've been trying to manipulate it, excel at it. I have systematically gone about competing with these seven tools.

Some criticize Anne's work saying anyone can do it. They cite its universality as its detractor. I suggest those people have a mistaken definition of the word universal when applied to acting. Something being universal doesn't mean anyone can do it well. It means it is affective to all people when done expertly. Not just anyone can do Anne's work expertly. To apply equal focus on the body and text at the same time takes rigorous concentration. This only comes with training, tenacity and a kick from the muse. Do not mistake these Viewpoints she binds a group of people with, as a code that unlocks a play. They are simply a test, watermarks to concentrate on reaching while discovering in the process what you are made of.

The discovery happens out of the moment that completely

and unexpectedly fails, and where you go from there. The View-points give you maps of the local terrain. They show you've nothing left but the other actors' breath and bodies as a way out or back in. It is in these moments you're never more possessed with love for your fellow actor: Aware they are you, their vulnerable big fat lie yours. It can be a moment of magic or unendurable closeness.

Someone I know says Anne puts furniture on the stage by way of the Viewpoints. It's a wonderful description. Whereas we cut our teeth in this country on love seats, the enigmatic "poof," the bench, the crate, the stump or bail of hay, what the director Anne Bogart gives you is the vast prairie of empty space. You, your body is the set. You're both moved and appalled at what this brings out in your partners, in yourself. With the two boards and the passion, however, come a very pragmatic set of issues on which to concentrate the body. The furniture is this physical structure.

In the best of rehearsals, the body's priority over the text allows a truer emotional response to surface. One is simply too busy to "act." When the body informs the psychology, the language is startlingly alive. The actor is available to a much greater range of musicality, and breathing becomes stronger, quicker.

I didn't understand those things that first summer. Anne suspected as much and had enough faith in me to let me figure it out myself. She's a balanced mix of someone unable to articulate much about acting and someone who knows that to talk about one's work is not interesting. She points at it. I put words to it. It is a rhythm that continues to sustain our friendship.

So we'd meet on the steps in the hour before the long rehearsal day began. We'd talked about our lives as unsettling presences in the world, loves, and whether I should quit smoking.

# 4.

As one loves the shore after shipwreck, I learned to love acting from a man named Tadashi Suzuki. He taught me nobility and the life and death nature it can assume far, far out on the edges of endurance. He takes you to a place you would not get to on your own. Ever. You do not go alone. You go out there to meet up with his relentless energy and vision. The passageway is the body. Once there you are connected with centuries of actors, all times, all cultures. The common link is the body. It's the only sure common denominator we still have. To stand on the stage, the actor needs to be an architect of time and space. As overwhelming as Mr. Suzuki's work feels from the inside, time and space are the only two issues you are consciously dealing with. He taught me there is a calm on the other side of razor-like concentration. He taught me courage simply by asking for it.

The director Anne Bogart's work on stage refuses to be any one thing. It refuses to find one image more significant or beautiful than another. What she is doing is developing an arena where the training of the actor has priority. Whereas Suzuki's "power tools" take high voltage on the actor's part to run and can have deadly results in crude hands, Anne's are the manual tools. They take a steady enduring energy to operate. Both require the same great attention to create the pristine angles and fine detail work in the finished product. If Mr. Suzuki taught me courage, Anne taught me innocence. To examine the unseen world you must look very practically at the body. While different, both structures that Mr. Suzuki and Anne offer offer freedom.

# 5.

Everyone is better looking than I am, I'm thinking. Even the guy playing Howard. Even the guy playing Bomber. It is the first rehearsal of William Inge's *Picnic* at Actors Theatre of Louisville. I'm hunkered down in my chair at the table, my glasses doubling as safety goggles to hide behind. I'm supposed to be Madge. The pretty one. I'm-only-eighteen-Madge the Newollah queen. I'm about to suffocate as I peek at Millie's dark hair and beautiful face. She smiles back a curious, warm hello. Diane D'Aquila playing Rosemary is all charisma, cheekbones and throaty laugh. I'm feeling like an asshole for feeling like an asshole.

I had called Anne after much agonizing to say I couldn't pull it off. I had another role offered and I was too old and really the role is all about how pretty Madge is...that's the point and won't the audience find it odd you've cast a Karl Malden lookalike and...silence on Anne's part. Then a quiet explanation about who she believes Madge is, and who she believes me to be. Think about it one more night, she says, and hangs up. The next day, regretting having to piss her off, I pick up the phone and am grateful to get her machine. Suddenly I'm saying I'll try. I'll be there. Yes. I hang up. What have I done? Why am I so frightened? I've been playing Agave for two years, a woman who's ripped her son's head off, for God's sake. What can possibly be frightening about this teenager from Kansas working in a dime store? What is frightening me is my own self-involvement, my literal-mindedness. If Suzuki has taught me anything, it is that art exists to hold back the tide of literal-mindedness in the world. I recognize the same urgent battle cry from Anne. I also know the sense of power and freedom I feel in Suzuki's work is now my responsibility to make every actor around me feel in Anne's landscape. If Suzuki reveals your depth of personal character, Anne reveals your ability to live the life of the imagination.

# 6.

The director Anne Bogart commences rehearsal for a written play with at least three solid days of table work. The text is explored line by line and actors are asked to come up with lists in response to specific questions Anne puts out. These lists are homework. You do them. They are read aloud, Anne pointing at random around the table. And she asks for not three or four choices written down, but fifteen or twenty.

That first day you come back with your homework, you are already responsible for the collective. Whether done half-heartedly or with pathological detail, whether the actor believes the process is helpful or not in those early days, you do them to keep up your part of the whole. Initially you think you can bluff your way through and sound like you know what you're doing. But no one knows what they're doing! That's the point. The choices you make are simply to shove the play as quickly as possible into deep waters. Or you think you can hide, which is equally as silly. The table work acts like a musical scale. You hear how each instrument around the room sounds against the same score. On one level you're hearing information about the other characters and how your role fits into the story. Mainly what you're hearing, though, is how the other people think, the tone of each other's creative energy. You familiarize yourself very quickly with the play and each other. You really can't hide. They help. Anne allows just so much time, and then the tables and chairs are shoved aside for good. The mopped and taped floor stands ready. Stage management, pencils poised, eagerly await the chance to start notating blocking. (Woe unto them! The clever ones haul out a video cam.) Now the ideas have to be translated into the body. Anne is a firm believer that rehearsal is not only an intellectual exercise, primarily it is a physical one. The fact that you have announced specific choices simply puts you immediately into action. You may abandon every initial decision in the end, but at the same time the oddest thing will come up weeks later. Usually in all the scraps of paper from the homework, there is a real diamond. It is usually something that came to you quite suddenly that goes on to become a cornerstone.

I've been in rehearsals where the answers given are barely audible, from a flushed and agonized face. I've also been witness to hour-long personal testimonies. In the end what really matters is that the body speaks. After all the table work, Anne promptly takes the text away.

Actors who've never worked with Anne often find in the initial viewpoint sessions a playfulness long since buried. Yet those same actors will approach the first whack at a scene with script in hand and pencil stuck behind ear. They are so used to the initial week being about putting meaning into the words, where the physical life amounts to well-coordinated page-turning and avoiding stabbing anyone with a #2. The next mistake is to believe that what she's asking is for you to mime the scene. What Anne is asking is that you build with your fellow players a physical life unrelated to the text; choreography with perhaps ten stops or moments that in and of themselves speak of a relationship. Not relationship as in lovers or enemies, rather a relationship to time, the surrounding architecture, physical shape...

Now, this is hard to do. Your brain says, "This is the moment in the scene when..." or "My character would do this because..." Exasperated, many of us turn to Anne. "I don't get this. Are we working on the scene or not?" Anne blinks from her perch. "Uh huh. Yeah. We're working on the scene. Now don't think about the text."

It's only after the choreography is refined and able to be concisely repeated that the text is laid in. The concentration needed to coordinate the juxtaposition of the lines with the movement occupies the actor. Depending on the *quality* of this concentration, the text begins to take on meanings one can't plan. You don't start rehearsals going for an emotion *you've* decided the play wants you to get at.

It can be awkward at first. Actors, fearing the ice a bit too thin, defend their discomfort. They claim the structures are claustrophobic because their backgrounds are based on realism. Phooey. A close observation of life (as Stanislavsky himself wrote) shows our physical life is more often than not contrapuntal to our verbal life. To recreate this realism takes objectivity and meticulous craftsmanship. It can be shocking to see how undramatic the process, through which illusion is created. Many actors' definition of realism amounts to nothing more than a high ground of personal habit (both mental and physical) retreated to under stress. They fail to see the composition as a much greater potential playing field.

The investigation of the internal world is pursued just as tenaciously. It is not an either/or situation. No feeling, memory or desire exists independent from the body on the stage. The form is the spirit. Acknowledging the obvious consideration that the audience both watches and listens, Anne is trying to provide for them by reestablishing a world where the body is as eloquent and articulate as the text.

# 7.

If you've ever tried to reach Anne by phone, you will appreciate that in Toga-mura, Japan, all I have to do is crunch through the gravel loudly enough to make her head poke out of her nearby window. We swap reports concerning our moods, what the day holds in store and, if I have time before rehearsals, I'm invited in for coffee. Private coffee stashes are precious in Toga, where the SITI company goes into the laboratory each summer. She shares hers generously. Once inside I survey her cluttered room. The floor is strewn with a profusion of books, clippings, computer printouts, journals and pictures. The private system of stacks and piles speak of present as well as future works, ideas taking hold. I touch a book with my foot and ask, "What's this? Why are you reading this? Who's this? Where did you hear of this?" That's how we frequently talk to one another, a bit brusquely, even suspiciously. As if to say, "Prove it, back that high-blown statement up, what does that mean?" She's as shocked at my conservatism at times as I am by her appalling lack of taste. I fail to recognize so many of her references as her conversation skips through past and present cultures. She, in turn, shows a naiveté toward what makes an event dramatic and is sometimes more curious about acting than caring.

These are our flip side perceptions, opinions we shuffle through as quickly as they come up. For if Anne lives outside acting, she operates with a freedom, a visa into actors' lives. She offers room to move with the unrelenting demands of a ballet master. Rehearsals blend the sensibility of improvisational jazz with the strictness of a Bach score. For some of us it is a chance to kick off our shoes and go nuts. It can be everything.

Anne sometimes says what drives her is her anger. In her paranoid, innocent, open ways I believe her only to the extent that anger is a byproduct of something bigger. What impels Anne is her ceaseless celebration of the individual. She establishes a very particular relationship to each actor she works closely with. It is through this private commitment, along with the box of gadgets she gives you, that an actor can begin to build a true sense of identity as an artist.

Standing in Anne's littered room in Toga, I wonder what possible lifetimes for me as an actor lay at my feet. Mahler booms in the background, competing with long passages of Marshall McLuhan which Anne is enthusiastically reading aloud. Pages from last night's script session unfurl from the printer. *The Medium* is being birthed by five intrepid SITI souls with Anne in lightning-flash days and exhausting nights. It is only later in New York I join this cast as a result of a prohibitive Equity regarding a European member. For now I enviously listen to clamorous table work and the bass line of Darron West's sound design pulse through the floorboards. Sampled from cyberjargon and McLuhan's own writings, the script taking shape looks ominously leaden. It's later I see the very energy and originality finally achieved comes from the previous life the words have had. Textually, everything is appropriated—and then reinvented by asking the simple question—What do you do with the meat? It's a question asked over and over again in Anne's plays.

She's just getting started. She's looking at the state of the art of acting and wants to talk about it, influence it. She's asking actors to unsentimentalize the self and to do hard things. It's that simple.

◆

I have discovered that the director Anne Bogart is an actor. She let me in on a secret and now I know we're pulled by the same current inside. When she's really stuck and the air's gone dead, when a group of baleful faces look back at her from onstage—she charges the space. Sometime between leaving the music stand and arriving on the boards, she's got to come up with a solution. It's like checking the parachute by leaping out of the plane. It's more fun that way. It's a breathless limbo stretch of seconds, when the mind races the heart. It's a dead heat finish for the director Anne Bogart.

◆　◆　◆

# Reflections on Anne

by Eduardo Machado

EDUARDO MACHADO IS THE PLAYWRIGHT WHO WROTE *In the Eye of the Hurricane,* produced as part of the 15th Annual Humana Festival of New American Plays and directed by Anne Bogart. His most recent play, *Floating Islands,* produced at the Mark Taper Forum, includes *In the Eye of the Hurricane* as the second of four acts of the production. His other plays include: *Once Removed, Fabiola, Broken Eggs* and *Across A Crowded Room.*

I first heard about Anne Bogart when she directed *South Pacific* at New York University (NYU). She set it in a mental ward, as everyone knows by now. At the time I was closely associated with a branch of the Oscar Hammerstein clan and spent a great deal of time with them at their loft in Soho. We would always go for long walks in the afternoon. One afternoon we began to notice posters of what appeared to be a show about Vietnam, and we were surprised it was called *South Pacific*. The poster featured an explosion, an Asian woman screaming and a very homoerotic picture of a G.I. We laughed and thought it was a joke, a spin-off on *South Pacific*, a new kind of review like *Forbidden Broadway* done by college students. After all, no one would seriously dare to toy with an American Classic.

Then one morning, after the show had run for a weekend, word got to the Hammersteins that it was indeed *their South Pacific*. Lawyers were called; "The production must be stopped!" But since NYU is so near Soho and everyone had heard this Bogart person was talented, the Hammersteins went to see the show...and they had to admit that it was the work of someone extremely talented. So the lawyers were told to leave the show alone. From that moment on, I decided that I had to work with Anne Bogart.

◆

When Actors Theatre of Louisville told me they would produce *In the Eye of the Hurricane*, they asked if I had any ideas for a director, and I said, "Anne Bogart." Up to this point I had never told Anne that I wanted to work with her and now Actors Theatre wanted to fly her in. I called a mutual friend, got her phone number, left a message and prayed she would call me back. (Anne is famous for not answering calls for weeks.) But to my surprise she called me back the next day. I told her the plans for the play. She came by my apartment and picked up the script. And I waited to see if she liked it.

Several days later she called and we set up a meeting to talk about the play. Actually what happened is that we began instantly to work on the production of the play.

When one has a first meeting with a director, they usually talk about what the play needs: better ending, clearer theme, editing. To my surprise, all Anne talked about was whether or not she would be able to breathe life into the play. She never asked for anything but that. It was shocking and still as I write about it today, I get goose bumps. It was a very warm and emotional moment in my life as a writer. I was totally charmed, because the one thing you must know about Bogart is that she can charm. She doesn't direct, she mesmerizes; the writers, the actors, the stage hands, the designers and the audience all fall to her hypnotic talent.

◆

Anne works on a play by choreographing moves driven by the actor, which begin to fill up the stage like a moving painting. Words are superfluous, it seems. And words to a playwright are everything. So there was a moment of panic. The script must depend on its own power to say its message, I whispered to myself. Actually, what the movement is doing is making the words live in a theatrical reality instead of a television reality. As the rehearsals continued I felt the most free I have ever felt as a writer. I spoke freely to the actors about what I wanted to say in the play and all of us together brought to life a moving, verbal, emotional song.

◆

Like all great theatre people, Anne is a magician. And magic is hard to really rationalize. I feel very fortunate to have collaborated with her on a moment of magic that was seen by the audience at Louisville. I hope in the future she will direct another one of my plays.

◆　　◆　　◆

# Making Up the Rules

by Charles L. Mee, Jr.

CHARLES L. MEE, JR. IS A PLAYWRIGHT AND AUTHOR OF *Orestes,* which was produced by the Saratoga International Theater Institute in both Saratoga Springs and Toga-mura, Japan. His play *Another Person is a Foreign Country* was directed by Anne Bogart and was produced by En Garde Arts in New York.

When we did *Another Person is a Foreign Country*—
which was about people on the margins of society and beyond—
we started without a script, and the first thing we did was drive
around looking for cast members. We discovered there was a
program on Long Island for people with all sorts of disabilities,
so we drove out to meet them, and Anne cast a young woman
with Downs Syndrome because the young woman wanted to be
in the piece. Anne didn't know what the young woman might
do, but that didn't matter. Some men who had been in a mental
hospital until recently all played musical instruments, so we re-
cruited them as a band. Several other people who had been institutionalized until recently read us their poetry, and we figured
we would put their poems into the script somehow. Anyway,
Anne wanted to cast Tom Nelis because she loves to work with
him; so we decided there would be a mad, inspired poet in the
piece, and Tom would play the poet. And we found a choir from
New York's Lighthouse for the Blind to sing. We found a woman
who had, from birth, almost no legs. The piece was produced
several years ago in New York by En Garde Arts, which special-
izes in "site-specific" work; and we did it in the courtyard of an
old abandoned nursing home. Down the block from the site
there was a home for elderly people—and a women there who
wanted to be in it, so we cast her and a boy from the neighbor-
hood. We composed the piece in the flesh, with people we
found, with the talents they brought to us.

Anne is well known for her warmth and empathy for other

people, for her greatness as a human being, for her ability to work with young actors or people who are not actors at all—as well as with trained actors—in a way that makes them feel secure to open up whatever they have to bring to the theatre and to flourish on stage. All of this often sounds, in the telling, simply like a description of what a wonderful person Anne is. But it's also what allows her to make a kind of theatre no one else makes.

The young woman with Downs Syndrome was able, finally, to sing a song—for which she got a great ovation every night. The boy danced. The band had such a good time, they often stayed on after the show, and sometimes the audience danced.

◆

Anne is able to do a really fine production of a standard American play that depends on the unfolding revelation of an underlying psychological destiny, that is bound by the preordained rules of psychology. But she is able, too, to do a piece that is simply composed of the people who perform it—or of an idea, of the inscape of Marshall McLuhan's mind, or of the American fad of marathon dancing. She can do a piece that is informed by a structure that is not psychological but that is intellectual, or political, or musical, or mathematical, or that creates its own structure as it goes—simply by responding to what is given, to what is found on the stage, in the performance itself. This is working without preexisting rules—or it is making up the rules as you go along; this is a true experience of how it is to be free—a rare experience—one to be felt, cherished, and applied elsewhere. Good directors can stage a play, can take what preexists and "realize" it. Great directors make pieces out of what happens on stage, without preconception, out of pure performance: that's what is really alive in a theatre.

Anne always puts me in mind of another of my mentors, the philosopher Richard Rorty, who insists that we do not discover the truth; we create it.

◆

This past autumn, she directed a reading of a screenplay of *The White Hotel* by Dennis Potter. The cast was lined up straight across the stage in front of a long table with water bottles set out on it. Five men in white tie sat to one side, ready to come forward from time to time to sing music of the twenties and thirties. A pianist to the right. An opera singer to the left, silent throughout the entire reading except for two moments when she sang two brief, heartbreaking pieces of classical music. Sounds from sources that encircled the audience. Unmistakably a reading of a script, but with one or two delicate touches—the singers, the soundscape—that lifted it into its own realm, and made the evening as satisfying in its way as a film or a play: a complete, unique work of art that existed only on that one evening.

◆

She can do things in the theatre that can't be done if you don't do them her way, the way Schoenberg can write a different kind of music than Gregorian chant because of the way he conceives music. He can get to different ideas, different emotions, different understandings of what it is to be human. That's the test, finally, of a way of making art—whether it is merely a manner or a style, or whether it allows us to know and feel something we could never have known and felt otherwise. Anne takes us places we've never gone before, where we cannot go without her. She opens up new continents to us; that's why we treasure her.

◆　◆　◆

# Creating a
# New/ Different America

by Tadashi Suzuki

*Translated from Japanese
by Leon Ingulsrud*

TADASHI SUZUKI IS THE FOUNDER OF THE SUZUKI COMPANY of Toga (SCOT) in Toga-mura, Japan, and co-founder, with Anne Bogart, of the Saratoga International Theater Institute. His work has received international acclaim and has been produced in theatres and festivals around the world.

I is difficult to write about Anne Bogart. The reason why it is difficult is simple: Anne is in the process of changing.

A director is one who betrays the expectations and prejudices of others, and through that very act of betrayal, creates new expectations. And as Anne is a director, it seems pointless if not dangerous to dwell on what one thinks the future holds for her. Likewise, to analyze the past would tend to imply that she is already finished with her work and that the rest is simply denouement to what has already come.

◆

The fact of the matter is that Anne Bogart is in a very interesting place right now. This is because of the battle which she is fighting. It seems to me that Anne is in the front of a battle in which all American theatre artists find themselves. So what is it that she is fighting? She is fighting America. What does she hope to win from this battle? Here again the answer is America. In a wonderfully energizing way she is caught in a paradox of shattering the very thing she loves in an attempt to discover it anew. To wake it up.

In specific terms, Anne Bogart is taking on the backbone of American theatre: realism, and the Stanislavski derived system of acting which supports it. By refusing to breathe the theatrical air that is so all-pervasive around her, she has created a vacuum that demands to be filled by something new. So what is the new/dif-

ferent America that she is looking for? This has not yet made itself fully known. There is much material which suggests features
of it, but this is material of the past, and as yet the true form of
this new image does not fully exist as a style outside of the fer-
tile mind of Anne Bogart. I truly believe that the best of Bogart is
yet to come.

There is definite proof of what is to come in the production
of *The Medium*. But whether the America that we see in this
production is the new/different America which she is trying to
create is an open question. It is, however, undeniable that there
is something new and American in this production, which theatre artists outside of America have long been wanting to see.

◆

It takes a great deal of time for the cultural activity of a
given nation to become visible to us as something indelibly
physicalized. It also does not take shape or become permanent
but through the talents of an individual. This is the essence of
how tradition appears in the arts. One must consider the work
and the vision of Anne Bogart within the larger context of theatrical history. What we see today may well only be the hints
and shadows of the larger impact that this work can have on
American cultural history.

It is my hope that Anne Bogart's talent and efforts will show
to us a new and convincing backbone for America. This will, in
and of itself, widen the horizons of world theatre.

◆　　◆　　◆

# Anne Bogart and the New Play

by Paula Vogel

PLAYWRIGHT, SCREENWRITER AND PROFESSOR, PAULA VOGEL has headed Brown University's Playwriting Workshop since 1985. Her most recent work, *Hot 'N' Throbbing,* opened at the Hasty Pudding, American Repertory Theatre in Cambridge in April 1994, directed by Anne Bogart and received the Fund for New American Plays Award from the Kennedy Center. Other plays written by Ms. Vogel include *The Baltimore Waltz,* also directed by Anne Bogart, *Desdemona,* and *And Baby Makes Seven.* An OBIE for Best Play, the AT&T New Play Award, National Endowment for the Arts Playwriting Fellowships, Bellagio Center fellowship from the Rockefeller Foundation, a McKnight Fellowship, and a Bunting fellowship are also included in Ms. Vogel's achievements.

PANELIST

*Under the Influence:*
*Anne Bogart's Impact on Collaborators and Critics*

Actors Theatre of Louisville
Modern Masters—Anne Bogart

# I.

My first argument with Anne Bogart was very one-sided. I spoke to her in my head as I watched *No Plays No Poetry*, her inaugural production at Trinity Repertory Theatre. The excitement I felt that night disturbed my sleep for several weeks to come. I was excited as much as by disagreement with her production as by agreement—for here was a director who provoked a dialogue with the audience, who invited disagreement and who left the play unresolved. Like many productions staged by the Wooster Group, her *No Plays* was an experience that had to be re-experienced and remembered by the spectator in order to be resolved. Today, several years after, my memory of her production constantly changes as well.

In fact, to watch *No Plays* is to remember not only Brecht, but Victor Shklovsky, the Russian Formalist from whom Brecht so artfully stole. Shklovsky's theory of "making strange" would become Brecht's Alienation-Effect. Shklovsky argued that over time our perceptions become "automatic" to us; we become so familiar with the route to work or an exercise routine that has become habitual that we no longer notice it. Thus, we are adept at driving a car when we are "automatic" and no longer notice the pedestrian we have swerved to avoid. The purpose of art, then, is to take familiar things and estrange or defamiliarize them so we notice the familiar once again: "My God, with the toe muscles of my right foot I am propelling one ton of metal down the street at thirty miles an hour a mere inch away from that pedestrian." Shklovsky quotes Tolstoy's diary to further illustrate how perceptions are "automatic":

> *I was cleaning a room, and, meandering about, approached the divan and couldn't remember whether or not I had dusted it. Since these movements are habitual and unconscious, I could not remember and felt that it was impossible to remember—so that if I had dusted it and forgot—that is, had acted unconsciously, then it was the same as if I had not. If some conscious person had been watching, then the fact could be established. If however, no one was looking, or looking on unconsciously, if the whole complex lives of many people go on unconsciously, then such lives are as if they had never been."[1]

"Art exists to make one feel things, to make the stone stony," says Victor Shklovsky.

To watch Anne Bogart work with an actor and a chair is to see both the actor and the chair in new ways: not only in the way that the chair is manipulated by the actor, but the way the actor appears to be manipulated by the chair. Bogart has the amazing ability in staging through a precise, plastic formalism to estrange the body of the actor while animating the furniture.

I wondered if Anne Bogart had meant to make Brecht feel more familiar (or, as Victor Shklovsky would say, more "automatic") through repetition in the second half of *No Plays,* which she staged in the downstairs proscenium arch theatre as a contrast to her invocation of the Alienation-Effect in the first half, when she estranged all of the theatre's devices by staging an environmental free-for-all in the lobby, the stairs, the dressing rooms and the lighting booth. We questioned acting, theatrical architecture, the audience's relationship to the action, the relationship of the theatre to the real. Shouldn't the order of the two halves of *No Plays* be changed? The first half to become the second half? Did the company, as its members worked on this piece, discuss when repetition causes estrangement, and when it starts to become too familiar?

The argument raged in my head in the aftermath of *No*

*Plays*. What would Brecht have said? Did Anne Bogart think she could only defamiliarize classic work? Contemporary writers can be allies in deconstructing their own work, too, I argued to the air as I watched her production.

"I'm right here," I repeated as a mental litany, as I trekked through the environmental spaces warring with each other in the lobby, the backstage, the scaffolding, the staircases. "You should really work with me. I'm right here. Five minutes across town. Work with me. Work with me."

It is the central irony of my career that Anne Bogart would indeed work with me—both of us as fugitives from Trinity Rep— she as the former artistic director, removed after only one brief year, me as the writer never allowed through its doors. Anne Bogart had announced, shortly before her own departure, that she would direct my play *The Baltimore Waltz* in her second season. For one day, the day of the press announcement, I walked through the front door of Trinity in my home town of Providence, not as an audience member, but as a playwright.

The night of the first preview of *The Baltimore Waltz* at Circle Repertory Company will remain a highlight of my professional life. I particularly remember the glow I felt, not after the reviews or after the audience response, but rather, the few seconds before that first curtain went up. For on the sidelines of the audience, stage right, I stood in the midst of a group: Anne Bogart to my right, Ronn Smith, the dramaturg, and Loy Arcenas, the extraordinary designer, to my left. For the first time in my theatrical experience, I was in the cave with my tribe, an included member, and we shared a group experience of pride in each other and excitement in our group accomplishment. Anne Bogart, among her many important contributions to the American theatre, excels most of all as a director of the new play, as a mover, shaker and shaper of newly-minted theatrical texts. By bringing her analytical eye, which deconstructs the theatrical text as a site of contradictions and multiple interpretations, to the work in progress, she is an ideal collaborator of the new American play. Her most exciting work has been done in the venue of plays by current and contemporary voices in the theatre: Mac Wellman, Charles Mee, Eduardo Machado and Laura Harrington.

Before explaining these claims, we must discuss some of

the problematic circumstances facing the contemporary American playwright now. I can tell you this—whatever our position is in this current moment in the theatre—it's not on top.

*"Did you hear about the (fill in the ethnicity of choice) actress? She slept with the playwright."*

# II.

FROM THE 19TH CENTURY THEATRE TO THE SCREEN:
THE DIRECTOR AS DOMINATRIX

In terms of prestige and influence within the theatrical process, and in terms of critical esteem, the position of the American playwright is at a historical low-point. On one hand, American theatre has been contaminated by the Hollywood studio system of production, so that commercial theatre is seen as fodder for theatrical films. Moreover, the process of producing the film has influenced the theatrical process. The Hollywood system, as well as the Hollywood movie, is the twentieth century regurgitation of the 19th century dramaturgical model based on the well-made play, or melodrama. The means of production resembles a director-run process modeled on the Duke of Saxe-Meiningen, the German Duke who reigned not only over his duchy but as the artistic director of the Meiningen players, and who exacted complete obedience and exercised rigid authority over his actors and designers, very much in the mold of Wagner. Wagner insisted that the director, as the visionary genius, should have control over all artistic functions in the theatre as a synthesizing force. From Wagner to Brecht, the model of the director as autocrat continues in the film and stage to this day. Brecht created the paradox of calling for the end to the *Gesamtkunstwerk*—Wagner's integrated work of art—while continuing to operate as the Master Artist, in the model of Wagner and Saxe-Meiningen. To change the production, Brecht knew, one must change the means of production. Thus, he called for the dismantling of the integrated machinery of Wagnerian production, or as he termed it, the separation of the elements—so that the text, gesture, sound, acting and lights of the production were no longer saying the same thing—yet he still modeled himself as the central authority, a director in the Wagnerian mold. Movies, we are told endlessly, are made by directors. Or to paraphrase David Mamet's comment about the position of the writer: "When they say in Hollywood that they want to collaborate with the writer, what they really mean is, 'Bend Over.'" This auteur theory of director has also corrupted the way plays are directed. In rehearsal the director becomes dominatrix. Scripts turn into products, written by employees, who are not included in the theatrical process of rehearsal and interpretation.

Following the Hollywood system, playwrights have become increasingly separated from the process of producing the play. Often our exclusion from rehearsals and the daily work of not-for-profit theatres is couched in reverential terms: rather than worry our pretty little heads about such things as budgets, deadlines and dirty work, we are saved for inspiration, creativity—or, in other words, for isolation. With similar rhetorical logic, so were middle-and upper-class women placed on the pedestal in the 19th century, saved from the drudgery of such things as voting, banking and running for office.

Anne Bogart offers instead the possibility of another model. A director of great gift and insight, she is developing the capacity to include the writer in the process of production. She is creating an atmosphere in the rehearsal room in which writers are seen as workers with the right to participate along with the actors, designers and interns. She offers a glimpse of another definition of the director-writer-actor hierarchy, layering the production with sites of resistance to one authorial intention. Bogart forges a dynamic which side-steps the eternal power-struggle between director and writer. The problem of collaboration comes from the misunderstanding of who is the author of the play. Or: who wears the theatrical pants in the family?

# III.

## THE PLAYWRIGHT IN THE PO-MO MOMENT

Academic postmodern theory also contributes to the disdain for playwrights. Theatre has always been seen in the academy as beneath contempt. Many of my colleagues who, while never having read Marie Irene Fornes, assume that all playwrights are creating *No, No Nanette* on the American stage. These same colleagues, who can not quite control the curl of their lips when discussing theatre, go into rhapsodies over Grade-B movies such as *Attack of the Killer Tomatoes*. As a healthy reaction to the reverential tone of New Criticism, which treated every word of the writer as an important hieroglyph in an as-yet-undiscovered Qumran Scroll, postmodern theorists have, perhaps, constructed the writer as an idiot-savant who has created her or his work unwittingly, serving at best to offer material for the true artist, the theorist, to deconstruct. And the less self-conscious the artist is, the more the work is rooted in popular culture, the better the work serves as a showpiece for the creativity of the critic.

Postmodern theory has contributed vitally to contemporary writers: notions of reality as construction, rather than the real; the awareness that all texts are battlefields of contradictions and that each work, when examined, implodes; that meaning is constructed not only by the writer, but by the reader as well. In the words of Catherine Belsey:

> *Composed of contradictions, the text is no longer restricted to a single, harmonious and authoritative reading. Instead it becomes plural, open to rereading, no longer an object for passive consumption but an object of work by the reader to produce meaning.*[2]

Let me clarify: I believe that the playwright authors the script, the director "authors" the production, and the play itself—that is, the meaning and sum experience of the work, the journey to interpretation—is written each night by each individual audience member.

The postmodern playwright, exemplified in this decade by such writers as Mac Wellman, Suzan-Lori Parks, Connie Congdon, Charles Mee, and Tony Kushner, follows Bertolt Brecht's dictum literally: we as playwrights are separating the elements. Only where Brecht was speaking as a director do we apply him to our new play dramaturgy. We expose the contradictions that we are aware of in the play as we write it (and rely on the process of production to further find and critique the contradictions we are blind to), we layer the work with multiple meanings, we defamiliarize closure. In other words, we separate the elements *within* the text.

Characters are no longer the neat sum of the "back story," to use a Hollywood word, added to the predicament, multiplied by plot and environment. The relationship of character as the combination of traits completely needed to motivate the action (thus, the rapist has the back-story of childhood abuse, the predicament of losing his job, the opportunity of the single woman living on the ground floor) has been abandoned as a formula by the postmodern playwright even as it is embraced as truth itself by the New York critics. In a postmodern play, character, plot, language, and environment or plasticity as self-contained entities correspond fitfully, if at all, and only until the playworld fragments once again. Kenneth Burke called the relationship between theatrical elements of character and plot, character and scenery "ratios."[3] Thus, Burke explains dramatic construction as a relationship between plot and character. The character of Willy Loman, for example, is constructed to contain and motivate the unfolding plot of *Death of a Salesman*; the plot of *Death of a Salesman* further changes and constructs his character. The notion that plot and character correspond symmetrically is best exemplified in the well-made play and method acting and by *L.A. Law*. Our great American playwrights such as Tennessee Williams and John Guare have long since severed the ratios, or correspondences, between action and character. Their female protagonists, such as Blanche in *Streetcar* and Betty in *Landscape of the Body*, have little or nothing to do with forming the action of the playworld from the recipe of their characters, and find themselves adrift in environments which act upon their characters with a ruthless machinery independent of psychology.

Mac Wellman in his profound, witty and ground-breaking essay, "The Theatre of Good Intentions," says it another way. Wellman calls the construction of "rounded" character, perfectly formed so that every trait matches an explanation or is revealed by plot, the "Euclidean character." He accurately dissects our current obsessions with pop psychology which have so permeated our drama that:

> *the plays of our time are, for the most part, so forgettable because their authors succeed all too well: a play that is a perfect and seamless summation of itself and its own intentions, and nothing else, can only be consumed once.*[4]

The great plays of our theatrical legacy, which we will never be able to consume once, e.g. *Woyzeck, Macbeth, The Baccae, Duchess of Malfi, Ubu,* and *Spring's Awakening,* deconstruct playworlds which, in analogy to their mirrored contemporary worlds, unravel their own making. Only our age, through the scrutiny of critics bound on consistency (the mark, we have been told, of small minds) and dramaturgical tidiness, insists that we produce new plays which remain "raveled," plays which are symmetrical, "feel-good" products for the consumer, and once consumed, provide carrion for subsidiary rights. I am reminded of the headline for the review of my recent collaboration with Anne Bogart, *Hot 'N' Throbbing,* in *The Providence Journal,* my local paper. It read: "Throbbing: Too Many Ideas." We are entrapped in a double standard for playwrights: one set of rules and expectations for living American playwrights, another set of rules for great European authors, preferably dead.

No wonder our great directors, our Bogarts and Akalaitises, our Woodruffs and Serbans and Ciuleis and Brooks, tilt at the windmill of the classics. Or they deconstruct the realist play through production of these stalwart staples of the American stage—as Anne Bogart has done in productions of *Picnic* or *The Women.* But another path is for living playwrights and living directors to work in collaboration with living designers and actors to expose the contradictions of our theatrical paradigm and the dominant cultural ideologies in the present moment.

Like all of us, I hold dialogue with the great American directors in my head as I watch them stage the bold and brilliant productions of Brecht, Shakespeare, Ford, Calderon, Jarry and Büchner: you are giving us great gifts—but please remember, that

Büchner will not write another play, informed by the brilliance of your production. The new techniques and collaborations you forge in the rehearsal hall must be shared with the living playwright. We are right here. Take us into the rehearsal hall, and into your rehearsal process.

So "who does wear the pants" in the playwright/director relationship? Let me offer a few appreciative comments about a director who took me into her rehearsal, into her process, into her plasticity.

# IV.

## DESIGNING WOMEN

One of the great advantages of living a life outside the comforts and restrictions of heterosexual orthodoxy is the necessity of questioning binary roles and terms and ideas: word pairs such as straight and homosexual, male and female, active and passive, woman and man, butch and femme, top and bottom, but most particularly, playwright and director. Those of us engaged in theatre, engaged in acting, writing, staging and designing, should be the ones most critical of the distinction between role and role-playing. There is no essential arrangement between playwright and director in terms of a hierarchical power and process, as there is no essential arrangement between husband and wife. Rather, there is a delicate negotiation for each writer and director collaboration which changes according to the play, the theatre, the company and the space.

Thus my relation to Anne Bogart and *The Baltimore Waltz* was substantially different the first time we worked together, as she staged the play in her living room, then as a piece in the laboratory at Circle Repertory, then with a different cast (with the exception of the wonderful Joe Mantello as The Third Man) for the main stage of Circle Repertory, and then again with the Houston cast at the Alley Theatre. At each incarnation, Bogart threw away previous spectacular blocking with a profligacy that speaks of her infinite invention; thus, too, Joe Mantello created a different Third Man opposite Barry Sherman and Melinda

Mullins than he did working with Cherry Jones and Richard Thompson. Anne Bogart created a different role for herself as director in each production, and I would hope I constructed a different playwriting role.

If I could articulate what I most appreciated about my first Bogart collaboration, it is that we didn't get married. There was no "fusing" of our aesthetics, an attempt to synthesize her interpretation to mine. Instead, she created an atmosphere in which we all were partners in the process, all playing our role but changing the air itself by our presence. Denise Yaney, the Circle Repertory stage manager, and the interns helped stage the way the sofa was used. The actors presented short tableaux according to Bogart's exercises during a brief but intense discovery period, which each of us in the room responded to as audience members.

I saw the production layered with different interpretations: now Bogart took the lead, then Cherry Jones. Next, my text came through, to be replaced in turn by the voice of Loy Arcenas. I would like to think, too, by my use of the actual words uttered while he was alive, my dead brother asserted his own resistance to my text. Rather than a synthesized *Gesamtkunstwerk*, Bogart coordinated more of a call and response dynamic of leader and chorus found in gospel music, a new leader changing from moment to moment, the chorus sometimes agreeing, sometimes resisting.

The greatest importance of Anne Bogart's work with living playwrights, as in *Baltimore Waltz*, is that she instinctively understands that to separate the elements of her production, to layer and fragment the meaning, she must incorporate sites of resistance to her own interpretation, whether it's the design, the performance or the text. Our greatest battle came in the tale of the sofa. I had written *Baltimore Waltz* with the image of a bed in my mind, acting as a platform which would be carried over the stage rather like Mother Courage's wagon over the landscape of Europe—a floating, transformational object which at times was the bed, at times a magic carpet, at times a bistro table—a bed which changed its function, like a good Russian formalist device should, in the same magically estranging way that as children my brother and I transformed our beds into tents, houses and forests.

No matter my argument, Anne and Loy saw the hospital lounge and its ubiquitous beige lounge sofa. And so, Anne won the battle—but the sofa floated, became the Eiffel Tower, became the bed—in our articulation of difference, she won the argument, but I felt that somehow, a bed floated on stage. Likewise, I could never have foreseen how my obsession with Strauss, with his *Emperor Waltz*, would find its way into her deconstruction of the waltz through the entire play, so that Carl and the Third Man became dance partners jockeying for the position of leading the dance, two men seeking which one will yield.

Anne Bogart allows the writers she works with to resist her meaning—and not only her living collaborators of Wellman, Harrington, Mee and Machado—for by incorporating their voices through stage directions into her productions, she has staged the resistance of Claire Booth Luce and George Kaufman to her interpretation.

Generously, Bogart also realizes that her interpretation of the living writer is only one possibility among infinite possibilities. Unlike many of her peers, who insist on a monopoly of interpretation, she shares new and living work with other directors. Remarkable contemporary work—such as Charles Mee's *Orestes*—may be seen through the eyes of Tina Landau as well. We do not have to wait one hundred years before Charles Mee is accorded the respect given to Büchner; we can learn from the different productions at Saratoga and under the West Side Highway. Bogart engages in a call and response with her peer directors, partaking in a dialogue about the contemporary writers she shares with other living directors.

I loved being in the rehearsal room at Circle Repertory with her, because she creates a room where everyone loves being. I loved hearing the responses from the twenty-year old interns at Circle, accorded the respect of Anne Bogart's inquiries. *The Baltimore Waltz* was a remarkable production because Anne Bogart created a remarkable process. I remember the day of the first preview, when we left the claustrophobia of the theatre to take in air, cigarettes and lunch. I returned to the theatre and found a design intern on Loy Arcenas' stage on her hands and knees, rubbing at a spot which was almost invisible. She had been that day an important contributor to the small adjustments in the technical rehearsals which are so crucial to the making of the production, and now she was spending her lunch-break inspecting the tile floor. I asked her what she was doing, and she looked up from her self-imposed chore. "It's got to be perfect," she said, "for Anne."

I look forward to an American theatre where every director treats their playwriting collaborator with as much respect as Anne Bogart gave to that intern.

◆    ◆    ◆

# Notes

1 "Art as Technique," Victor Shklovsky, in *Russian Formalist Criticism, Four Essays*, Lee T. Lemon and Marion J. Reis, eds. Lincoln: University of Nebraska Press, 1965, p. 12.

2 "Constructing the subject: deconstructing the text," Catherine Belsey in *Feminist Criticism and Social Change*, Judith Newton and Deborah Rosenfelt, eds. New York: Methuen, Inc. 1985, p. 54.

3 I apologize for the immense simplification of Burke's analysis of plot-character and scene-plot ratios, and his superb contribution to dramaturgy with his notion of *dramatism*. I have relied constantly on his first and second chapter of *Grammar of Motives*, as well as his elegant essay, "Psychology of Form." And I thank Bert States for introducing me to the work of Kenneth Burke.

4 "The Theatre of Good Intentions," Mac Wellman, *Performing Arts Journal*, V. 21, p. 64.

# ◆ CRITICAL POINTS ◆

# The Meat of the Medium:
## Anne Bogart and
## the American Avant-Garde

A commentary
by Porter Anderson

A MEMBER OF NEW YORK'S DRAMA DESK, PORTER ANDERSON is the former standing theatre columnist for *The Village Voice* in New York City and managing editor of *The Islander,* the weekly newspaper of South Carolina's sea islands. He's an Advisory Council member of the American Theatre Critics Association, a past Vice-President of the International Association of Theatre Critics and has written on theatre and/or dance for *American Theatre, TheaterWeek, Dance Magazine, The Sarasota Herald-Tribune, The Tampa Tribune, The Dallas Times Herald, The Pittsburgh Post-Gazette, D Magazine, The Dallas Observer, Profiles, Spirit, Sky, American Way, Interview* and *The World Book Encyclopedia Year Book.*

## KEYNOTE LECTURER

*The Meat of the Medium:*
*Anne Bogart and the American Avant-Garde*

Actors Theatre of Louisville
Modern Masters—Anne Bogart

*Now Eros shakes my soul,*
*a wind on the mountain,*
*falling on the oaks.*

    —Tennessee Williams' quotation of Sappho,
    affixed to his script of *27 Wagons Full of Cotton* [1]

"What do you do with the meat?"
Anne Bogart tells me she loves that question.
"What do you do with the meat?"
You may wonder if anyone else among us is finding it as mildly titillating as you find it—well, just to dispense with one possibility, it's not a reference to the comely fact that her performance company members have trained so rigorously in her own and Tadashi Suzuki's movement techniques that they've got the shapeliest calf muscles in the business.
But you're warm.
And the question, for Bogart, is not rhetorical.
She's asking.
She's asking you.
Here.
Now.
In every single show of hers you see here in Louisville during this late-century *fête de La Bogart*, in every gesture of her actors' agility, in every viewpoint through which she sizes you up—and she is sizing you up—Anne Bogart is asking.
"What do you do with the meat?"
The question is more urgent than entertaining, more serious than it sounds.
Don't sit back and relax.
Sit forward and be tense.
When Bogart asks "What do you do with the meat?" she's speaking to you from what journalist and author Douglas Rushkoff calls *Cyberia*.[2] C-y-b-e-r-i-a. As in cyberspace.

I'm sure you're familiar with the concept of Virtual Reality.

In its most popular commercial manifestations to date, of course, Virtual Reality is something about plaid young people and sweater-ed college teaching assistants all donning gadget-y helmets and joystick-y gloves so they can have the illusion of being inside a video game. And at that level—located somewhere in the shopping mall imagination between the films *Tron*[3] and *Total Recall*[4] (good calf muscles on that Arnold Schwarzenegger, too, maybe he knows Suzuki)—Virtual Reality all seems to be merely a lot of harmless human young dragons in dungeons of petty circuitry. No wonder one of the most popular, if not very Virtu-ous, entries in the field of late has been the hot-selling game "Doom II."

But Virtual Reality, as you might have suspected, has currency far beyond a PacWoman's[5] wealth and our own jealousies of the youths who nowadays take to this technology as avidly as turtle hatchlings head for the sea.

It's much more.

Bogart has found Cyberians asking, "What do you do with the meat?" as they message each other about new Virtual programs, E-mail each other about new computer-interface devices, romanticize on the 'net[6] with each other about new levels of electronically enhanced consciousness.

They're asking, "What do you do with your body?"

The answer, for some, is torso and whole-body suits, not just helmets, not just gloves, so that computerized stimulation and imagery and fantasy—transmitted by modem or microwave from a stranger or a most intimate cyber-buddy—can become teasers and tormentors to your complete battery of organic receptors.[7] They're hooking up as many electrodes as surgical adhesive will stick to their nerves. They're stripping down and then wiring up their bodies so that a stroke of the character **T** on a keyboard in Portland will be felt as a caress by a thigh in Sacramento.

Soon, the technology will get lighter, you know, the electrodes might be implanted, you know, only the head's, not the whole body's, nerve clusters need be wired and even then maybe not hardwired, you know, but simply bathed in blue-white showers of orgasmic stimuli—by remote control.

As Bogart has the one whose screen name might have been

Marshall McLuhan say in *The Medium*:

> *If you're good-looking and got the dough, you're going to have sex with beautiful women for real. If you're lonely and introverted and have no dough and a crummy apartment, you're going to have Virtual sex with fake beautiful girls.*[8]

Reach out and touch some body.

That's what they do with the meat.

That's what they plan to do with the meat.

That's what *they* already are well on their way to doing with the meat.

But Bogart is still asking.

Still asking the question.

"What do *you* do with the meat?"

◆

Is the problem that she didn't hear the answer?

No.

The problem is that you haven't come up with it.

She's got the Cyberians' answer. And she's online with it too, finding our American lives here, today, in the incipient suburbs of cyberspace as intriguing as she finds other forces looming about us. In fact, for a hint at just how widely interested in life Bogart is, let her pick you out something in a bookstore while her beloved Tina Landau[9] searches out high-grade suspense novels: Bogart will take you over to the audio books (don't forget to get batteries for your Walkman) and she'll hand you tapes of *The Tao of Physics*[10] and Alvin Toffler's *Powershift*.[11] Not for Bogart, the theatre section only, she's wandering around Barnes & Noble's stacks with the business babies, the philosophes and the politicos, too.

But "What do you do with the meat?"

Why does she keep asking that question?

What answer is she waiting for?

What answer is she waiting for you to give her?

"What do you do with the meat?"

◆

Anne Bogart is something more immediate than a contemporary classic, more of this moment than a modern master. She's a present classic. She loves to talk of "present memory."[12] "Theater," she says, "gives us the present of memory...present memory...distanced yet close. A *mise-en-scene* can jolt and disturb and delight and *remind*," she says. "We can become *mindful* of new signs in our culture, around us. We can meet in the theatre to confront ourselves with our society and reflect upon influences."

And, of course, in Bogart's new *Small Lives/Big Dreams*, Kelly Maurer—who embodies the spirit of Chekhov's *The Cherry Orchard*—says, quite early on:

> *Don't lag behind.*
> *To live in the present, we first have to make up for*
> *our past, to have done with it once and for all.*
> *Be as free as the wind.*
> *Marvelous visions of the future.*[13]

Predictably for someone who does have marvelous visions of the future and who is taking such care to help us make up for our past, Bogart is a present classic whose context is mercurial. It's not what it was 10 minutes ago. It's not what it will be 10 minutes from now. Like mercury, so liquid a context is quicksilver at best, quicksand at worst, and as ephemeral as the fiberoptic impulses that fizz and evaporate in the luminous dreams of hovering young Cyberians. Presumably, Jon Jory has called us here not just to praise her but to place her in the American avant-garde.

And yet to do so might be both to praise her and to bury her.

After all, what life do we allow our artists of what's called the avant-garde in this country? Not for nothing did Bogart tell writer Catherine Sheehy years ago, "I usually personally resent being called avant-garde because I spend most of my time thinking about history, tradition and culture."[14]

Sad to say, of course, an American who does think about history, tradition and culture *is* avant-garde. And, if we accept this to be the case, we might just stop right here, declare the American avant-garde to be vested entirely in Bogart and go home.

But, obviously, a few people who wear an awful lot of black clothing and never venture west of the Hudson or north of 28th Street are going to challenge that move.

So our first problem in fixing Bogart's relationship to the American avant-garde is trying to define the American avant-garde.

As fearful as any other term is to us from outside our own language, the phrase *avant-garde theatre*—meaning the advance team, if you will, someone ahead of the pack—conjures up in most Americans' minds either:

- "weird stuff," by which they mean experiments in theatrical form, or

- "political stuff," in which they fear that American and/or Confederate flags will be burned by naked and probably homosexual Asian, Hispanic or African-American females who do not accept Jesus as the Great Schehungene.

As Robert Heinlein wrote, "One man's religion is the next man's belly laugh."[15]

So let's take "weird stuff" first.

The form question.

◆

The average American's disinterest in the exploration of form in the theatre is the reason that the majestic histori-scapes of Robert Wilson are making most of their glacial, elegiac progress in Europe, not here. New *Wilsonwerks* light the lights of Hamburg. And the United States doesn't know what it's missing. And doesn't care.

That same disinterest is the reason that Martha Clarke has taken her gift for creating gorgeous nightmarish Music-Theatre Group spectacles such as her *Vienna: Lusthaus*[16] and *Miracolo d'Amore*[17] and *The Garden of Earthly Delights*[18] and *The Hunger Artist*[19] offshore—to Jiri Kylian's Dans Theatre of the Nederlands for which she's creating an evening-length version of her *Dammerung*[20] and to the Royal National Theatre in London where she's collaborating with playwright Christopher

Hampton[21] on a new approach to *Alice in Wonderland*.

When Clarke ended up with a weak text of Walt Whitman poetry for her piece about Nazism, African slavery and environmental crises, that work, which was titled *Endangered Species*[22,] lived right down to its name's warning. It was closed early, slammed by bad reviews and no-show audiences—and this happened, a few years ago, at no less a temple of forward-looking theatre than Harvey Lichtenstein's Brooklyn Academy of Music in New York in its Next Wave Festival, theoretically a home for the avant-garde.

When Robert Wilson's adaptation of Georg Büchner's *Danton's Death*[23] spewed its French Revolutionary heresy at Houston's Alley Theatre just a couple of miles from where George Bush was ceding the presidency on election night, 1992, the mainstream national news media were surely there, positively crawling Houston to watch the Democrats' artificial resuscitation of that three-headed monster, Liberté-Egalité-Fraternité. But the press took absolutely no notice of the elegant parallels that Wilson had installed in a kind of staged chiaroscuro of glowing, jewel-like sculptural pieces and bravura performance. Two heads rolled in Houston that night. The Americans cared only about George Bush's long-overdue decapitation and were open to no such timeless and timely a context as Bob Wilson offered them.

When Julie Taymor's horrific and lovely puppetry images came to Lindsay Law's *American Playhouse* on the Public Broadcasting Service, achieving what looked like neo-Breughelism in *Fool's Fire*[24]—a glory of greased-peasant fairytale cruelty— the news wasn't about the unprecedented vision she offered the country but about how PBS had transmitted to its affiliate stations a "soft feed," meaning a slightly edited version that might not offend any Christian terrorists who happen to channel-surf across Taymor's airwaves on their way to *Murder, She Wrote.* Heaven forbid they discover a puppet muttering, "I say there is no arse-wiper like a well-downed goose." That's the line they edited. Those are the words they feared.

When Jawole Willa Jo Zollar's Urban Bush Women raised the roof of their 1990 theatre piece called *Praise House*[25] under the "light-painting" of designer Leni Schwendinger's umbrella-elegant imagery, they couldn't even fill the house with Americans interested in seeing so eerie an exploration of the "outsider artists" of the rural South, people who, like Minnie Evans and James Hampton, draw and paint religious iconography in trance-like, fevered states of rapture.

And you'd be wrong to get excited when crowds flocked to George Coates' Performance Works in San Francisco for *Box Conspiracy: An Interactive Sho*,[26] despite the fact that it's a "very avant" production of multimedia projections.

They were there because they got to wear 3-D glasses.

And that's entertainment.

If you say that experimentation with theatrical form is the "avant-garde," you'll find that in the national mind you've spoken of everything from a three-stools-and-black-turtlenecks *Hamlet* to the entrance on a Jeep of the four-story-tall *Warrior Ant*[27] of Lee Breuer or the harbor-side driving-range ghost-angels of Tina Landau's *Stonewall: Night Variations*[28] or the grass-wandering ghosts of Meredith Monk's *American Archaeology #1: Roosevelt Island*.[29] And the term "American avant-garde" has become a Virtual oxymoron: Americans outside a very few urban centers like New York, Los Angeles and Chicago, have so little point of reference in theatrical form to begin with, that formal experimentation is moot among their interests.

Americans liked *Harvey*[30] a lot. A lot of them are still looking over their shoulders for tall rabbits. If they don't see them when they line up at a box office, they're not happy: all else is "avant." Even the most stylistically aggressive musical on Broadway—commercial theatre's theme park—is a revival, a revival of *Carousel*,[31] no less, the 1945 Rodgers and Hammerstein clambake that asserts that if a woman really loves a man it won't hurt when he hits her.

No wonder, then, that more than 11 years ago, Bogart wrote, "The tendency of the New York avant-garde toward self-referential theatre, narcissistic and autobiographical, is a product of a society that glorifies the cowboy, in this case an individual isolated not only from others but from his or her own history."[32]

Funny, isn't it, how both cowboys and *Carousel* start with a C.

So does Cyberia.

Anne Bogart's business is about something much more than

theatre's self-reference...or -reverence. Wilson, as she has noted, "is wonderful at facile spectacle."[33] But it's in Wilson's Europe, where she found her inspiration in the work of such *auteurs* as Peter Stein[34] and Ariane Mnouchkine,[35] that she learned to try to connect form to culture and social ideas.

"I think that our struggle as Americans, myself included," she says, "is with content. Therefore, it's my intention to ignore form as much as possible, because I know it's going to be there, and focus on content."[36] And this is one of the great inspirations of the Viewpoint Training she has developed for her actors.

Since we're talking of theatrical form, let's note that there are now nine "viewpoints," she tells me,[37] not the earlier six she has used in developing her actors' vocabulary of physical presence on the stage. The nine viewpoints are:

- spatial relationship,

- shape,

- kinesthetic response (one actor to another—this one's my favorite, you'll see it manifest remarkable, hurtful and quite beautiful power in *The Medium*, when the impact of an energy seems to slam into one body, then ripple to the next and the next and the next),

- repetition,

- gesture,

- architecture,

- tempo,

- duration, and

- topography.

Having trained her artists to apply these nine viewpoints in their presence on stage, Bogart then goes about setting a work very tightly, meaning that she's what some theatre artists would call a "dictatorial" director, the deliberate opposite of the director who encourages actors to "do whatever feels right for this moment in the script, darling."

Darron West's[38] ravishing soundscape for Bogart's new *Small Lives/Big Dreams*, for example, has very few running cues, he tells me, contrary to the multiplicity of cues for *The Medium.* And these two shows have been made, remember, a year to 18 months apart, during which time Bogart's sense of her directorial "Viewpoints" has matured and been tested in several very confirming productions. In the last two years in particular, she says, she's refined her commitment to rooting her actors' stage life in movement, drawing on American 20th-century modern dance and Asian studies related to Suzuki's highly athletic, stamping work. So thoroughly and precisely choreographed is *Small Lives/Big Dreams*, West says, so locked-in is each performance, that—not to ignore the weeks and months of preparation needed for his score—a couple of long tapes are all he needs to play the entire show's sonic work. It's that dependably set.

This will sound un-American to many in our theatre industry, but Bogart's specific goal is to free her theatre of the curse of the American Method developed from the Stanislavsky system.[39]

In order to achieve any emotional life on stage, she believes, the structure of a work must be concretized. Once that happens, the artists will have their physical bearings so confidently moored that they can be open to the tides of human vulnerability that make for rich dramatic life.

For a memorable example of this, watch Maurer's *Cherry Orchard* performance in *Small Lives/Big Dreams*—when she knows precisely when and how she's to sit on the basket of belongings she has placed at a meticulously determined spot downstage left in the final moments of the show, when she knows utterly at what angle her spine is to hold Andryevna's regal head and at what counter-angle her hands may sag with Firs' inertia, then she's freed to deliver her lines with uncompromised attention to what they mean and how they feel. She says this:

*I'll only take a minute. How odd, I can't find it any-*
*where... Can't remember. Yes, life here is over and*
*done with. ...Last year at this time it was snowing.*
*Remember? We must be going. It's time. On our*
*way! I remember when I was six years old. Now*
*that's what I call licking the glass clean. Goodbye*
*to our old life. My life, my youth. I have to move*
*on. There's not much time. We're coming. We*
*should be on our way. It must be time to go.*
*Yoohoo! It's time to go. No strength left.*[40]

And at the end of that speech, Maurer's still sitting—after all,
Bogart likes to draw on Asian philosophy and say that in order to
get something, you have to do the opposite.

"And it was Stanislavsky who first understood," Bogart says,
"that in order to create a real moment on stage, you have to
think about 90 different things. His approach was psychological.
This has permeated the theatre of our century to a point that I
find unbearable. But the principle is right. You can't just walk
on stage and be actual or be authentic. The Viewpoints are
things that the body and the mind can 'think' about to actually
take your mind *off* 'being natural.' "[41]

And so when it comes to experimentation with form—the
"weird stuff" side of what Americans think of as avant-garde theatre—Bogart is working to free *us* of the very forms we love by
setting them as firmly as she directs, in precise stage interpretations, so that we can look at these forms, think about them, *feel*
what they mean to us, what they've meant to us and why we
cling to them. Her trilogy of shows about early-20th-century
American entertainment forms, the first two installments of
which have been *American Vaudeville*[42] and *Marathon Dancing*[43] and the third of which will deal with silent films, are efforts to make us look at a black-faced minstrel down on one
knee and a Depression-era dance marathon with such boisterous
life and intelligence and objectivity that we can then turn and
ask the harder emotional, subjective question: How was it that
we could possibly have seen entertainment on such a stage just
a moment ago, just a decade ago, just a generation ago? What
were we thinking? Weren't these "traditional entertainments"
nothing more than institutionalized euphemisms for suffering?

What did we do with the meat?

Bogart's *A Streetcar Named Desire*[44] used ten Stanleys and twelve Blanches to break her audiences free, for a moment, of the Brando image of Stanley.

What did we do with the beefcake?

Her *South Pacific*[45] was played in a hospital setting as therapy for battle-shocked war veterans. And, with the producing support of Anne Hamburger's site-specific company En Garde Arts, she set the little people and apparently hearing-impaired artists and otherwise "handicapped" souls of Charles Mee's *Another Person is a Foreign Country*[46] in a moonlit, abandoned building called The Towers on the Upper West Side in New York, a former cancer hospital and later a torturously corrupt nursing home, a structure designed in the 19th century by architect Charles Coolidge Haight as what looks like the quintessential gothic asylum.

What did we do with the mind?

What Bogart did and does with mind and body, with the meat, with the humanity of her artistry, is present it in what writer Eelka Lampe calls her "aesthetic of disruption"[47] in order to rescue it from the norm and free it from our all-too-traditional love of emotional indulgence, rank sentiment.

"We are," Bogart writes, "dangerously seduced by imagery and exterior appearances [in the theatre]. ... We slip continually back into 'using' the audience as passive consumer[s] of presented art. Many possibilities for vicarious and indirect audience participation have not yet been explored."[48]

She's exploring them.

"I didn't go to Japan" to work with Suzuki in Toga "to try to understand or mimic another culture," she says. "I can't understand it, I can't mimic it. I went to learn more about American culture, by looking at it from the outside."[49]

And yes, the "weird stuff" of her experimentation in theatrical form may be what some would call "avant-garde" with a sneer, but it's one way she's looking for something to "do with the meat."

Because she's still asking.

"When I was doing *The Women* in San Diego," Bogart tells me, "we had a second preview—and the theatre [San Diego Rep] is in a shopping area, you know, basically in a mall. And the actors were on stage in this matinee performance doing incredibly fabulous work, and the audience was totally dead. And I got so depressed. I said, 'What do I have to do to work in regional theatre?' But later, I realized that I was looking at this thing the wrong way. It's not an audience that I'm looking for, it's *part* of an audience that I'm talking to. It's not that I can't have an audience that goes to theatre in a mall, but that I'm trying to reach a part of them, a part that can hear what I'm saying. And sometimes that part won't be there or won't listen. The question is not 'Who is my audience?' but 'What part of any audience am I working for?' "[50]

I submit that by being here today, you're very much part of the audience she's working for and talking to.

And what she's saying to you is, still, "What do you do with the meat?"

♦

And what of the other major common assumption about American avant-garde theatre?

"Today, when theatre in the United States makes an attempt to address social issues," Bogart has written, "it is labeled 'political theatre' and relegated to a special corner of the field."[51]

It's in that corner that you might expect to find Bogart most deeply ensconced, having gotten a heavy dose of political medicine early.

She's a Navy brat.

Her maternal grandfather was Admiral Raymond Ames Spruance, Task Force Commander at the Battle of Midway in June 1942, Commander of the 5th Fleet in 1944, Commander of the Pacific Fleet in 1945 and United States Ambassador to the Philippines from 1952 to 1955. Bogart's father at one point was in charge of the Norfolk Naval Air Station and her family was moved around in her childhood, both to assignments in this country and to such distant ports as Tokyo.

So there's no surprise in her voice, just explanation, when she tells you these days why she developed her production liaison with Suzuki three years ago—she learned as a kid that she could get some perspective on the United States by leaving it for a while and looking back.

Make no mistake, her and Suzuki's Saratoga International

Theater Institute program is no happy marriage of their two *aesthetic* natures. "They are philosophically linked in their desire to change the status quo," Steven Oxman has written, "but their artistic sensibilities are quite distinct." Both Suzuki and Bogart focus their critiques of contemporary theatre on the limited scope of naturalistic acting "facsimile acting."[52] But just get Bogart into a corner and ask her to do her impression of Suzuki—whom I've heard some around her call "Suzi Q"—her impression of him asking an actor, "Why you so bad?"

Yes, Suzuki's a tough taskmaster, even an authoritarian in the way he works with his performance artists, Bogart concedes. "But somebody has to do his kind of work," she says, likening it to the Ballet Russes, so forceful is it in performance, so sturdy in its presence, so unflappable at its homebase of Toga where fireworks and spectacle are a large part of the allure, that "in a way," she says, "his work is invulnerable. It doesn't matter who the audience is. His work is just there. And nothing can blow it off the stage."[53]

For her own part, she's looking for something much *more* vulnerable—and, as she revealed in her comments about the San Diego Rep audience, she's therefore having to *accept* a lot more vulnerability in terms of how she's received. It *does* matter to her, if not to Suzuki, who the audience is because she's searching for contact with, access to, at least a part of that audience.

And, sure enough, Bogart's got critics always ready to try to blow her stuff off the stage.

*New York Newsday*'s Jan Stuart once wrote, "There is no middle ground in an Anne Bogart production. Those who do not walk out cursing the director in foreign tongues are exhilarated."[54]

You couldn't ask for a better demonstration of this than last spring's response to the arrival of *Marathon Dancing*, which was assailed by *The New York Post*'s Clive Barnes under a headline blaring "Skip This Endurance Contest." Barnes leveled at her the crass dismissal, "Oh, well, They Shoot Dogs, Don't They? Bye, Fido." Michael Sommers of the Newhouse papers called the staging of *Marathon Dancing* "incredibly moribund," *The New York Times'* Ben Brantley said it was "fiercely cynical" and "one-note" and *The Village Voice*'s Michael Feingold talked about how the show traded in "used goods."[55]

As Mel Gussow so succinctly observed in *The New York Times*, "Depending on the point of view, she is either an innovator or a provocateur assaulting a text."[56]

For *The Boston Globe*, Clifford Gallo wrote up the initial incarnation of *Cinderella/Cendrillon*,[57] Bogart's interpretation of Massenet's opera, stating, "For all of the emotion expressed in the crystalline vocals and in Cendrillon's anguished dilemma, the cumulative effect...is strangely icy."[58] But when Bernard Holland took to the pages of *The New York Times* about it, he came out with this remarkable lead: "Advertisements for the Music-Theatre Group's *Cinderella/Cendrillon* at St. Clement's Church on Thursday night were enough to chill the opera lover's spine. A 'retelling' of the Cinderella story with 'a modern sensibility,' they promised. ('Retelling' plus 'modern' in small American opera companies usually means 'vulgarization.') Selective editing, adaptation and additions to Massenet's little-known opera were also announced (for these three processes, read in most cases 'perversion and destruction'). The production—shared by Anne Bogart, Jeff Halpern and Eve Ensler—began with yet another scarcely tenable position: dialogue in English, singing in the original French. The rest of this review must devote itself to figuring out why it all worked so well."[59]

In writing up Bogart's Brechtian walk-through, which was titled *No Plays No Poetry But Philosophical Reflections Practical Instructions Provocative Prescriptions Opinions and Pointers From a Noted Critic and Playwright*,[60] Erika Munk wrote of how "An officious person...herds the audience here and there, setting up healthy resistance." She went on, later in her article, to write, "Being ordered around so much seemed like a satirical jab at early Schechner[61] productions."[62] Taking things an entirely different way, Gussow wrote in the *Times*, "Repeatedly the audience is encouraged to wander in various directions. We can choose from an array of instructive events... ." Indeed, the faithfully insightful Gussow, comparing *No Plays No Poetry* to other environmental shows of the season—which included the uptown *Tamara* and the downtown *Tony 'n' Tina's Wedding*—ended by writing, "*No Plays No Poetry* offers no dinner no drink. It alone provides food for thought."[63]

No one is more confused than the American public, of course, by the disagreements of critics. While London's theatregoers all but pile into their intermission bars to see if Wardle[64] might pick a fight with Coveney,[65] the American flock seems to think that critics should chant "Go" or "Don't Go" instructions in convenient harmony, if not solid unison.

Probably my favorite line from a raft of Bogart reviews was written by Pat O'Haire for *The Daily News* in a review of Bogart's interpretation of Wedekind's *Spring Awakening*.[66] Summing up Bogart, who's one of the industry's most compassionate and composed feminists, O'Haire wrote: "She's a lady with a vision, no doubt about it; I can hardly wait to see what she's cooking up for next year."[67]

With criticism like that, to paraphrase Daniel Schorr, may such artists as Bogart forgive us our press passes.[68]

Munk, however—whose review of *No Plays No Poetry*, I should note, was largely admiring—did get off a striking observation at the end of her article: Brecht was, she wrote, "above all a political writer. [And] *No Plays No Poetry* is non-political at heart, only half the equation."[69]

And there, Munk had put her finger on something that can confound and even disappoint many observers. Bogart isn't willing to stay at the political end of the American concept of the avant-garde. In fact, she rarely heads for the outright political at all. In the more than 60 productions with which she's been involved in the last dozen years, few have been as overtly and traditionally political as her *1951*[70] about the McCarthy hearings or her staging of Charles Mee's *Orestes*,[71] which pulled some of its imagery from the Beltway, set as it was on the lawn of the White House after the 1990 Persian Gulf war.

She's got bigger things in mind.

So if the "avant-garde" in this country means to people something that's either the "weird stuff" of formal experimentation or the "political stuff" of old street theatre, they won't find Bogart where they expect her to be.

Listen and you'll hear her, still asking:

"What do you do with the meat?"

◆

Anne Bogart was born in the same year that:

- the North Korean forces broke through the 38th parallel and Picasso painted *Massacre in Korea;*

- Peron was re-elected president of Argentina;

- Julius and Ethel Rosenberg were sentenced to death for espionage against the United States;

- J.D. Salinger wrote *The Catcher in the Rye;*

- The country produced 400,000 pounds of penicillin;

- Salvador Dali painted *Christ of St. John on the Cross;*

- Rodgers and Hammerstein's *The King and I* went to Broadway;

- Andre Gide died; so did Wittgenstein; Matisse did not;[72]

- John van Druten wrote *I Am a Camera,* which would inspire *Cabaret,* and Tennessee Williams wrote *The Rose Tattoo;* Christopher Fry wrote *A Sleep of Prisoners,* Benjamin Britten wrote *Billy Budd,* Igor Stravinsky wrote *Rake's Progress,* Frank Lloyd Wright designed the Friedman House in Pleasantville, N.Y.; and

- Color television was introduced in the United States. So was Anne Bogart. The year was 1951.

She was born in Newport, Rhode Island, not far from Providence, a place that several decades later would prove less than providential when she took over the Trinity Repertory Company there for one mean year.

You may know of her experience there. Briefly, she was appointed by the board of Trinity Rep, one of the nation's more visible and better-respected regional-theatre houses, to succeed the founding artistic director, Adrian Hall. It was Hall, poignantly enough, who would tell me a few years later as he directed *As You Like It* for the New York Shakespeare Festival in Central Park,[73] that the American regional-theatre system is, in fact, a myth.

Both Hall and Bogart, while vastly different artists, have had similar experiences in regional theatre as its interest in serious art crumbled and was replaced by the country's rising appetite for entertainment.

Hall was censured at both Trinity and the Dallas Theater Center for being too aloof from sponsors, for being disinterested in the "donor-schmoozing" side of the job and for spending too much money on shows. Bogart was pushed into resigning when the Trinity Rep board demanded that she cut her production budget by a quarter, from $4 million to $3 million—and this, after she'd already announced an ambitious second season and had spent a year of her life wading through the byzantine petty politics and pseudo-corporate constraints that most of the country's institutional theatres nowadays try to hide from you backstage.

Even while still president of TCG, or Theatre Communications Group, the national service organization of regional theatres, Bogart began speaking quite bravely and passionately of how marketing directors seemingly do the play selection in these 300 or so not-for-profit theatres once touted as the future of the art in America.

And just this past year, TCG's own annual survey of American regional theatres began to confess with new clarity to an awful, downward momentum in theatre that few can deny anymore:[74]

- 42 percent of the surveyed theatres, TCG revealed, have operating deficits, 22 of them in excess of $100,000, three of them exceeding $1 million each—in fact, in five years, TCG's sampling of theatres has gone from a $1.2 million surplus to a combined $5 million deficit;

- nearly half the surveyed theatres are reporting declines in attendance;

- subscribers continue to fall away;

- federal grants have dropped 8 percent in just one year;

- local grants have plummeted 13 percent in the same year;

- regional theatres are closing at a rate of about five per year; and, most importantly of all,

- new-play development has dropped 65.7 percent in five years. That's new American play development, once the most hallowed mission of the regional theatres. Down two-thirds. In just five years.

Why aren't you hearing more about this? Many mainstream critics are afraid to write truthfully in their publications about what's happening to the art of live theatre in this country—they know they'll lose their jobs if their editors realize that auditoriums are half-empty and that the overwhelming majority of readers have little or no interest in live theatre.

But in *American Theatre* magazine, despite that publication's understandable efforts to paint the regional-theatre system as a bustling network of community-engaged drama, TCG's Barbara Janowitz wrote last April with admirable candor of how the American audience has become "a VCR culture where instead of making a commitment ahead of time, the film of one's choice is available at any hour of the day or night, with no charge for parking or babysitting; a culture that is placing more emphasis on dining and entertainment and less on the arts; a culture that is neglecting to adequately educate its children in many ways, including in the arts."[75]

Picture a group of cyber-aged youngsters, like those who hang out at a middle-American 7-11 in Eric Bogosian's new play, *SubUrbia*.[76] As they stand around "chilling" in the parking lot, they start thinking of things to do. Imagine one saying to another, "Hey, let's go see a play," let alone, "Let's put on a show!"

If our session right now were suddenly interrupted by someone off the street who strode up to me here, asked what I do for a living and heard me say I'm a theatre critic, there's every chance the response would be: "Oh, you review theatre? Great. What's a good movie to see?" This exchange really happens as the very word *theatre* is co-opted by the industry that should call itself cinema. And our theatre artists, all too many of them, become ever more panicked and pander to the movie-muddled mind with less challenging, more sitcom-y works to keep the box office alive. The *point* of it all gets harder and harder to find in what Bogart calls our "present memory."

Actors Theatre of Louisville is an exception, not the rule. And even Jon Jory has to balance what he does in such summits of serious work as the Classics in Context program and Humana Festival with mainstage series of more populist works.

And this is why, finally, Anne Bogart's position in the shrinking American theatrical nation is so unique.

She is not of the for-profit commercial theatre.

She is not of the not-for-profit regional theatre.

And she is not of the formal or political norm of the avant-garde, either.

I asked Bogart, very recently, just what it is that her theatre *is* about.

And here's what she said:

"I become more and more aware that there is one thing I have to say in theatre—I feel that every play I do has to ask the question, 'Why do we need theatre?' I realize that it's been true for years for me. It's actually my only true statement. I'm interested in the body, the human body that is the stuff of live theatre. For me it's the body, it's the meat."[77]

The message is the medium.

The medium is the meat.

What does *she* do with that meat?

- Well, she cyber-pummels it in *The Medium*, in which West's soundscape gives you the young Dionne Warwick singing the body electrified—*When will I know, where will I, how will I learn who I am?* (Apparently, of course, Warwick, since that recording, has had all those questions answered by her Psychic Friends Network, stepping right around the need for computers, as it were, and accessing the ether directly.)

Counterpointing Warwick's ballad of addiction, the McLuhan character says in *The Medium,*

*Man must, as a simple survival strategy, become
aware of what is happening to him despite the at-
tendant pain of such comprehension. The fact that
he has not done so in this age of electronics is what
has made this also the age of anxiety. But despite
our self-protective escape mechanisms, the total-
field awareness engendered by electronic media is
enabling us—indeed, compelling us—to grope toward a consciousness of the unconscious, toward a
realization that technology is an extension of our
own bodies.*[78]

- In Elmer Rice's 1923 *The Adding Machine*,[79] Bogart is dealing with a Mister Zero she knows very well. He's an early
victim of computational tyranny, a low-number ancestor of
the coming digital dynasty.

- And in *Small Lives/Big Dreams*, Bogart has surprised herself, by her own admission, to find that she has an apparently innately futurist vision even of the past. "I have this
theory about plays," she has said, "that they're little pockets
of memory. Like a Greek play about hubris—if you do it now,
it's a chance to bring that question into the world and see
how it looks at the time you're doing it. We've lost the sense
that theatre has this function of bringing these universal
questions through time. Now we think it's all about invent-
ing, making everything new. But how can you create something if you don't have anything to talk about but
yourself?"[80]

In *Small Lives/Big Dreams*, Bogart wants to know what the
insecurities that Anton Chekhov knew at the end of his century
can tell us about our own insecurities at the end of our century.
"There will come a time," says the composite character from
*Three Sisters*, "when everybody will know why, for what purpose, there is all this suffering, no more mysteries. The music is
so gay, it almost seems as if a minute more and we'd know why
we live, why we suffer."[81]
Anne Bogart is looking for that minute more.

She's asking for that minute more, on behalf of theatre.

She's trying to buy some extra time for this collapsing art of theatre, so quaint a little has-been of an art in techno-America, the sort of thing that the big yellow buses one day will take schoolkids to at various museum-theatres around the country— the 50 or so regional theatres that survive, like plate-spinners' halls of fame—to help our students learn about the "living TV" that preceded cyberspace, a funny old custom of earlier generations of people who would cram themselves into dark rooms to watch other people act things out under colored lights on cardboard sets.

Broadway, of course, already has left the field of art, with the lasers of *The Who's Tommy*[82] having pushed the entertainment-driven, profit-defined commercial theatre right on into what playwright Erik Ehn calls "the foothills of cinema" where plays are produced as "stunted movies."[83]

And what's left in regional theatre is looking all too much the same—*Tommy*, after all, started at Des McAnuff's La Jolla Playhouse, a regional theatre.

◆

Just as Bogart confesses that the message of her medium *is* that medium, I propose to you that Anne Bogart's work is the meat of what's left of the medium of American theatre.

In Anne Bogart, we find the meat of the medium, the most substantially challenging and most generously vulnerable mirror being held up to us from our stages.

In her "present memory," she gives you a way to enter this ancient art, in fact, as the secular cathedral it once was in other cultures, in other places, in other times.

As director Margaret Booker said to me recently, theatre is something we brought into the States from our ancestral societies—the arts and allures of cyberspace are native to us.[84]

"What do you do with the meat?"

What *will* you do with Bogart, with her work, with the work of this artist of such meaty perceptions and expressive power?

I'd like to think that the dwindling number of Americans who still distinguish serious theatre from entertainment might gather around Bogart to form a protectorate for her work. As Peter Brook has his Bouffes du Nord Theatre and International Center of Theatre Research in Paris, as Mnouchkine has her Cartoucherie as home to her Theatre du Soleil, also in Paris, as Suzuki has his mountainside development and performance center at Toga, as Wilson may some day have a similarly dedicated site at Watermill, Bogart needs *sanctuary*. She needs a place to which we all can make the pilgrimage—as Suzuki's audiences travel for up to two days to reach him. Her Saratoga International Theater Institute, or "SITI," as it's called, however ably produced it is by Jennifer Dana, isn't the answer, at least in its current state. Because SITI doesn't maintain its producing home in the City. As graciously as Carolyn Anderson's Skidmore College program has hosted SITI's efforts so far, Saratoga Springs may make sense as a summer home to Bogart's artistry, but not as the ultimate ground of her development. She needs something more central to the remaining American theatre audience and that, whether we non-New Yorkers like it or not, means something in New York City. She needs something with a lease as long as the Joseph Papp Public Theater has, with pockets as deep as Lincoln Center has, with an agenda as determined as Actors Theatre has.

I hope for Bogart the *sanctuary* she deserves, a place to make that "pocket of memory" she knows theatre can be.

But I fear she may not get it.

She's surrounded by theatre people today who say, "Oh, the theatre has faced threats to its existence since before the time of Christ and it's never been defeated yet so it's not going to be defeated now."

They're wrong.

Never before has theatre tried to pull its audiences from living rooms in which Sting can be watched in a live concert simulcast on television and radio by satellite from Berlin, then captured and manipulated, if desired, on CD-ROM.

In talks with artistic directors around the country, as a matter of fact, I've found that Jory is among the few who know and are willing to admit that the quickening demise of the art that so many theatre people steadfastly deny is something to which they've actually contributed. They've failed to carve out and content themselves with a niche of serious, society-reflective live theatre like Bogart's. They've gone instead for the same entertainment sell as Hollywood, for its glamour, for its bucks, for its stifling banality that reassures the maudlin majority.

American theatre today is a place of *Small Lives*, indeed, being lost to the *Big Dreams* of the Cyberians.

And so it's only natural that the Saratoga audience cracked up with a wicked-rueful kind of laughter last September when, in the American premiere of Bogart's *Small Lives/Big Dreams*, they heard these *Seagull*-winged lines:

> *Our theater is in a rut—it's so damn conventional. The modern stage is nothing but an old prejudice, nothing but a sad and dreary routine. They strive to squeeze out a moral from the flat, vulgar pictures and the flat vulgar phrases, a little tiny moral, easy to comprehend and handy for home consumption. In a thousand variations, they offer me always the same thing over and over again. I run and keep on running as fast as Maupassant ran from the brain-crushing vulgarity of the Eiffel Tower. But the stage is certainly an important factor in culture. We must have new formulae. That's what we want. And if there are none, then it's better to have nothing at all.*[85]

And there it is.

Bogart's question.

"What do you do with the meat?"

Is it better to have nothing at all than to have 90 percent of our country's stages filled with last year's Wendy Wasserstein hit and the previous season's Paul Rudnick comedy and the prior decade's Neil Simon yukker and a kitchen-sink drama revival that's more about the sink than about what goes on in the kitchen, all topped off with a modern-dress, nontraditionally cast Shakespeare and a Cole Porter revue?

As Chekhov watched the approach of the 20th Century, at least he was spared reading a Phillips Media advertisement in *Spin* magazine for a Virtual Reality game promising to "fuse a cyberpunk action-adventure movie with a frenetically paced role-playing game."

This is an advertisement for theatre.

In cyberspace.

And you're the star.

The program being advertised is called *Burn: Cycle*. And the ad is so theatrical, perhaps unwittingly, that it goes on to read like a cathode-ray marquee: "Hardwire your neurons—critics are calling *Burn: Cycle* 'a totally synthesized, fully transcendental, bio-controlled, electronic rush.'"[86]

Some of my sister and brother critics used to write things that ecstatic for Sondheim.

So what do you do with the meat?

What *will* you do with the meat?

Anne Bogart's work is superbly poised between the formal experimentation and political experience of the avant-garde, between hot tradition and the coolest-blue cyber-potential, between survival and extinction—theatre's own survival and extinction.

If you've cared enough to make this pilgrimage this weekend to Bogart's temporary home here in Louisville, I hope you'll take Bogart's question as a personal challenge. Because if that question is left to the vagaries of the nation's decimated arts-funding infrastructure, if Bogart's work continues to pop up here and there in one brave regional theatre's excellent adventure in the "avant," then in Toga, then in Saratoga, then in New York, then in Houston, then in San Diego, then again in Toga—her rightful artistic home never will be achieved, her Cartoucherie never will rise, her Bouffes du Nord never will open.

And as playwright Ehn writes, even moviegoers these days "develop a sometimes psychotic fascination with the whereabouts of actors in the flesh—with the drama of the bodies."[87]

To tone and honor the growing body of Bogart's work, we must guard against too glibly naming her a classic in the context of the "American avant-garde." If we relegate her to that popularly dismissed field, we scatter the focus of her culturally based work too widely.

As she says, her work is all about one question: Why do we need theatre?

"What do you do with the meat?"

Here, from the text of Anne Bogart's *The Medium* are the words of one fearsome answer to that question:

*I think you have to take the point of view that certainly the planet is the cradle of mankind but, inevitably, one cannot remain in the cradle forever. The human imagination, in conjunction with technology, has become a force so potent that it really can no longer be unleashed on the surface of the planet with safety. The human imagination has gained such an immense power that the only environment that is friendly to it is the vacuum of deep space. It's our own ingenuity and inventiveness that guarantee that this environment must now be superceded. The world rendered as pure information not only fascinates our eyes and minds but also captures our hearts.*

*We feel augmented and empowered.*

*Our hearts beat in the machines.*

*This is Eros.* [88]

# Annotations

1 Sappho, as quoted in Tennessee Williams' *27 Wagons Full of Cotton*, written in 1994, published in 1945, made into the film *Baby Doll* in 1956, as referenced in "Swinging Back for a Look at the One-Act," *Arts & Entertainment* magazine, February 1990, Anderson. Anne Bogart has said in interviews that Tennessee Williams is among her favorite playwrights.

2 I recommend Douglas Rushkoff's *Cyberia: Life in the Trenches of Cyberspace* to anyone who wishes to, to paraphrase Seattle's Intiman Theatre founder Margaret Booker, live in our time. Not only is Rushkoff's obvious joy and research in such topics as "technoshamanism" and "artists in Cyberia" infectiously theatrical, but also the dust jacket of the book is a shameless pop plastic pleasure to be cherished in guilty secret. And with an introduction titled "Surfing the Learning Curve of Sisyphus," you know you're not dealing with chopped liver.

3 *Tron*, 1982, directed by Steven Linberger and starring Jeff Bridges, Bruce Boxleitner, David Warner, Cindy Morgan and dear Barnard Hughes. It's Disney's thing about a "computer whiz" (Cyberians were still called that in 1982) who gets stuck inside a big computer and has to fight for every electrode he's got in a video game. Bridges is left to depend on the kindness of Disney's special effects people.

4 *Total Recall*, 1990, directed by Paul Verhoeven and starring Arnold Schwarzenegger, Rachel Ticotin, Sharon Stone, Ronny Cox, Michael Ironside and Marshall Bell. Here we get a lot closer, actually, to Rushkoff's vision of where we're going in cyberspace—Arnold goes to a commercial cyber-vacation outfit which peddles the 21st Century version of mental holidays in which computer stimuli create utterly believable journeys, all in the mind. Of course, everything's complicated because Arnold doesn't know he's a former secret agent whose natural memory has been erased by The Agency and he ends up on Mars and... never mind. The whole thing is based, by the way, on Phillip K. Dick's

short story "We Can Remember It for You Wholesale." Now, is that a cool title, or what? We could use a few nonmusicals on Broadway with titles so forward-looking and clever. For that matter, we could use a few nonmusicals on Broadway of any kind whatsoever.

5 PacMan was the Adam, if not the Eve, of the Eden that became Nintendo's garden.

6 Internet.

7 See Rushkoff's *Cyberia*, Chapter 4, "Interfacing With the Technosphere."

8 *The Medium*, 1993, Saratoga International Theater Institute, conceived and directed by Anne Bogart, based on the life and predictions of Marshall McLuhan.

9 Tina Landau, in the summer of 1994, wrote and directed *Stonewall: Night Variations* for Anne Hamburger's En Garde Arts site-specific producing company in New York. Also for Hamburger, she directed Charles L. Mee Jr.'s *Orestes*. Her *1969* was seen in the 1994 Humana Festival of New American Plays at Actors Theatre of Louisville. She directed *Marisol* (José Rivera) for La Jolla Playhouse, Daphne DuMarier's *Rebecca* at Trinity Rep and she wrote and directed *States of Independence* with composer Ricky Ian Gordon for the American Music Theater Festival.

10 *The Tao of Physics*, Fritjof Capra, Ph.D., 1975, 1983, and recorded in abridged form in 1990 by Audio Renaissance Tapes, Los Angeles, distributed by St. Martin's Press, New York. You listen to it with your eyes tightly shut and your mind wide open.

11 *Powershift*, Alvin Toffler, 1990 and recorded in the same year by Bantam Audio Publishing, a division of Bantam Doubleday Dell, New York. It's the end of Toffler's trilogy, the first two installments of which were *Future Shock* and *Third Wave*. In this one, Alvin goes to great lengths to belatedly thank his wife for her apparently integral contributions to all three books. He says she wanted no credit. But now he's decided she really must be thanked. Sounds like a powershift for sure, no?

12 You can read these and other comments from Bogart on this concept of "present memory" in her prescient manifesto, "Stepping Out of Inertia," published in *The Drama Review*, Vol. 27, No. 4, 1983. What you'll

learn in this short, three-page work, is just how clearly Bogart was sensing, a dozen years ago, what was then—and would be now—important to her in her work. We should all be so clairvoyant.

[13] *Small Lives/Big Dreams*, 1994, Saratoga International Theater Institute, conceived and adapted from the five major plays of Anton Chekhov and directed by Anne Bogart with the SITI company. World premiere, Toga, Japan. American premiere, Skidmore College, Saratoga Springs, N.Y.

[14] Interview with Catherine Sheehy, August 1990, text provided by Saratoga International Theater Institute.

[15] *Time Enough for Love*, 1973, by Robert Heinlein, G.P. Putnam's Sons and Berkley Medallion Books, New York. This is Heinlein's novel of "the lives of Lazarus Long," a die-very-hard whose lifetime spans from World War I to the year 4272, an exhilarating romp of a book that has all the best earmarks of Heinlein's bracing ability to break you out of our 20th-to-21st-century "present memory" and put you into some enchanting future mindset. Like Arthur C. Clarke, Ray Bradbury and Frank Herbert, Heinlein had the gift of making sense of our time and past by imagining our future. He wrote not science fiction but philosophical speculation, sometimes on an impressively elevated, energetic level. His focus was greatest, of course, in *Stranger in a Strange Land*, but just about everything he produced after, say, the earlier efforts of *Starship Troopers* (so there's a little space cadet in all of us), makes a worthy diversion, even today.

[16] *Vienna: Lusthaus*, 1986, Martha Clarke, with Music-Theatre Group.

[17] *Miracolo d'Amore*, 1988, Martha Clarke, in association with the New York Shakespeare Festival and Spoleto Festival U.S.A. My favorite of Clarke's works.

[18] *The Garden of Earthly Delights*, 1984, Martha Clarke with Music-Theatre Group, inspired by the Hieronymus Bosch triptych. The popular favorite in her canon.

[19] *The Hunger Artist,* 1987, Martha Clarke, based on the work of Kafka.

[20] *Dammerung*, 1993, set by Martha Clarke on Gary Chryst for "NDT3," Dans Theatre of the Nederlands 3, USA premiere at the American Dance Festival, Durham.

[21] Christopher Hampton is the British playwright best known for his *Les Liaisons Dangereuses.* He also has written *Total Eclipse, Treats* and other works, as well as adaptations and translations of others' titles including von Horvath's *Tales from the Vienna Woods,* featured in the 1991 Classics in Context Festival at Actors Theatre of Louisville. His and Clarke's collaboration on the *Alice* material is in the developmental workshop phase in London.

[22] *Endangered Species,* 1989-1990, Martha Clarke, in association with Music-Theatre Group, the Brooklyn Academy of Music and Circus Flora (St. Louis). For articles on the work's development, see *The Berkshire Eagle*, August 5, 1990, and *TheaterWeek* magazine, October 15, 1990, both Anderson.

[23] *Danton's Death*, 1992, Robert Wilson for Gregory Boyd's Alley Theatre, Houston. The original work, Georg Buchner's *Danton's Death*, was written in 1835. In his Houston production, Wilson worked against the kind of white-hot worlds that Giorgio Strehler is known to produce and developed a dark, inner upstage proscenium against which to silhouette the statuesque work of actors Richard Thomas (Danton) and others. For more on the production and the peculiar political setting of its premiere in Houston, there's a full review, "A Ravishing Ugliness," in *The Village Voice*, November 24, 1992, Anderson.

[24] *Fool's Fire*, 1992, by Julie Taymor and designer G.W. Mercier, a version of Edgar Allen Poe's *Hopfrog* in which Taymor drew from the writings of the 14th-century monk Rabelais. For more on this instance (among many, unfortunately) of PBS censorship, see *The Village Voice*, March 24, 1992, Anderson, Teasers and Tormentors theater column.

[25] *Praise House*, 1990, a production of Urban Bush Women, Jawole Willa Jo Zollar artistic director, text by Angela DeBord, music by Carl Riley, choreography by Pat Hall-Smith. Review-features of this work appear in *American Theatre* magazine, September 1990, *Dance Magazine*, October 1990, and *The Village Voice*, November 26, 1991, all Anderson.

[26] *Box Conspiracy: An Interactive Sho,* 1993, written and directed by George Coates, music by Marc Ream, scenic projections by Stephen Joseph. This piece, created at Coates' Performance Works in San Francisco and staged at Spoleto Festival U.S.A. in 1994, purports to explore a future in which society is offered 5,000 television channels. While positioned as a cautionary fable of techno-encroachment on our collective

humanity, the piece is in bad faith, utilizing endless stage-tech gadgets (not to mention the 3-D glasses to help you see the multiscrim projections' depth) and thereby mounting a truly vulgar display of precisely the hyper-theater hardware against which it warns. For more on this production, see *The Village Voice*, June 21, 1994, Teasers and Tormentors theater column, and *The Islander*, June 2-9, 1994, both Anderson.

27 *The Warrior Ant*, 1988, Lee Breuer and Bob Telson, Spoleto Festival U.S.A.

28 *Stonewall: Night Variations*, 1994, Tina Landau, En Garde Arts.

29 *American Archeology #1: Roosevelt Island,* 1994, Meredith Monk.

30 *Harvey*, Mary Chase, 1944, the loving-hands-at-home comedy in which Elwood P. Dowd talks with an imaginary 6-foot-tall "puka" or rabbit, and teaches everyone with whom he comes in contact to be real nice. It won the 1944 Pulitzer, for God's sake. Only in America.

31 *Carousel*, a 1945 work, opened in its new revival on Broadway at Lincoln Center, in the Vivian Beaumont, in the spring of 1994, a production of Lincoln Center Theater by arrangement with the Royal National, Cameron Mackintosh and, of course, the mighty Rodgers & Hammerstein estate. Its Douglas Hytner staging with Bob Crowley's designs takes it to a sort of futuristic Thornton Wilder-esque image of starry nostalgia and gently abstracted settings, making the revival something that most Broadway-goers who see it will consider quite "avant." But don't forget that most Americans who see their first staging of Wilder's half-century-old *Our Town* today will call its umbrellas-and-step-ladders business "avant," too.

32 *The Drama Review*, 1983, previously cited.

33 *The Village Voice*, December 18, 1984, an interview with Don Shewey.

34 The work of German director Peter Stein, particularly at the Berlin Schaübuhne, is known for two major areas of effectiveness—he pours vast research into contemporary topics to mount such pieces as his *Vietnam Discourse* in 1969 at the Munich Kammerspiele, and he uses a highly objective approach to classics to reveal their contemporary relevance, as in his *Three Sisters* of 1984.

35 Three years Stein's senior, Ariane Mnouchkine is the French director whose Theatre du Soleil performances in Paris have developed into a "people's theater" of huge, meticulously crafted classic-based masterworks, epics re-interpreted through filters of the most demanding Asian influences and requiring massive powers of vocal and physical performance from her artists.

36 Catherine Sheehy interview, previously cited.

37 Unpublished interview with Anne Bogart, August 13, 1994, Anderson.

38 Darron L. West, sound design for *Small Lives/ Big Dreams* and *The Medium*, also *The Treatment* for the New York Shakespeare Festival, *The Devils* at New York University, *Jennine's Diary* and *A Body of Water* at Circle Rep. West also has worked as a resident sound designer with Actors Theatre of Louisville. We spoke about his work on September 24, 1994.

39 Konstantin Stanislavsky, 1863-1938, the Russian actor, director and producer whose system of acting still undergirds the American approach to naturalistic stage playing and TV/film work. It was termed "the method" when Lee Strasberg and his Actors Studio modulated it in New York in the 1940s and the earliest and best-known emissary of the American Method was Marlon Brando. It's thanks to such "methodists" that acting students to this day are standing around in dimly lit studios and acting classes searching their bowels for the "feelings" their characters should experience, in this "organic"—as opposed to "technical"— way of working. Some of the more famous detractors of such an approach have included Laurence Olivier and Helen Hayes, both of whom were candid enough to say, at various points in their careers, that they preferred more technical access to their characters over an emotional immersion in their roles. And theater-training lore has produced several classically recited examples of the great "organic-technical" debate, one such supposed dichotomy being the work of the Italian Eleonora Duse and the French Sarah Bernhardt, both contemporaries of Stanislavsky. Duse today is said to have been a near-priestess of "internal," "organic" technique and Bernhardt a flamboyant gold-digger of the "external," "technical" way of working. This stuff is all but hypnotic to stage-struck trainees and can bedevil and sidetrack them for years of otherwise useful training time.

40 *Small Lives/Big Dreams,* previously cited.

[41] Unpublished interview, Anderson, previously cited.

[42] *American Vaudeville: A History in the Form of an Entertainment*, 1992, Anne Bogart and Tina Landau, premiered at Houston's Alley Theatre.

[43] *Marathon Dancing*, 1994, Anne Bogart with a text by Laura Harrington, produced by Anne Hamburger's En Garde Arts. *Pittsburgh Post-Gazette* critic Christopher Rawson felt that Harrington's script was too banal for Bogart to overcome; I felt that the banality was precisely the stuff of which so maudlin a spectacle as a dance marathon was made. Bogart, who is a lady and a diplomat, says both of us are right.

[44] *Sehnsucht,* 1982, Anne Bogart's adaptation of Tennessee Williams' *A Streetcar Named Desire*, Abia Theatre, Northampton, Mass.

[45] *South Pacific*, the 1949 Rodgers and Hammerstein musical, in a 1984 production by Anne Bogart, Mainstage Theatre, New York University Tisch School of the Arts. Ten years ago, you might be interested to know, the Rodgers and Hammerstein Organization wasn't nearly as interested in veering from the fathers' original concepts as it has been with the *Carousel* that Mackintosh ferried from the Royal National to Lincoln Center. Executives of the R&H Organization have conceded in interview comments with me for the League of American Theatres and Producers' *Broadway Presents* that, indeed, they're realizing they must begin to loosen up a bit on what they'll allow in interpretations of the shows as time goes by and as the shows get older and as even community theaters begin to look for *some* new way, *any* new way, to solve a problem like Maria.

[46] *Another Person Is a Foreign Country*, 1991, Charles L. Mee Jr., staged by Anne Bogart for En Garde Arts.

[47] "Collaboration and Cultural Clashing: Anne Bogart and Tadashi Suzuki's Saratoga International Theatre Institute," Eelka Lampe, *The Drama Review*, Vol. 37, No. 1, 1993. Extremely fine work, this article. Lampe clearly is a devoted champion of Bogart's work.

[48] "Stepping Out of Inertia," *The Drama Review*, previously cited.

[49] Comments made by Anne Bogart to the audience for a Suzuki-Bogart technique demonstration workshop, September 24, 1994, Saratoga International Theater Institute, Skidmore College, Saratoga Springs, N.Y.

[50] Unpublished interview, Anderson, previously cited.

[51] "Stepping Out of Inertia," *The Drama Review*, previously cited.

[52] Steven Oxman interviewing actor Eric Hill in "A Place to Create and Contemplate," *American Theatre* magazine, November 1992. Hill played Cadmus in Suzuki's *Dionysus* and Menelaus in Bogart's *Orestes* in the first season of the Saratoga International Theater Institute's productions at Skidmore College and the Saratoga Performing Arts Center in Saratoga Springs.

[53] Unpublished interview, Anderson, previously cited.

[54] Jan Stuart, "Bogart in Bali Ha'i," February 1985, *American Theatre*.

[55] This unhappy but amusing collection of criticisms was put together in *The Village Voice*, March 29, 1994, the Teasers and Tormentors theater column, Anderson.

[56] *The New York Times,* March 12, 1994.

[57] *Cinderella/Cendrillon*, 1988, based on the Jules Massenet opera, Anne Bogart and Jeff Halpern with text by Eve Ensler, directed by Bogart, produced by Lyn Austin and Diane Wondisford's Music-Theatre Group, first in Lenox, Mass., as *Cinderella in the Mirror*, then in New York City as *Cinderella/Cendrillon*.

[58] *The Boston Globe,* August 11, 1987.

[59] *The New York Times,* January 17, 1988.

[60] *No Plays No Poetry But Philosophical Reflections Practical Instructions Provocative Prescriptions Opinions and Pointers From a Noted Critic and Playwright*, 1988, based on the theoretical writings of Bertolt Brecht by Anne Bogart with Otrabanda, the Talking Band and Via Theater.

[61] Richard Schechner, to whom Erika Munk refers here, founded the Performance Group in New York and worked as a committed theater experimentalist whose best-remembered staging probably is the *Dionysus in '69*.

[62] *The Village Voice*, March 29, 1988.

[63] *The New York Times*, March 31, 1988.

[64] Irving Wardle, *The Sunday Independent* (London).

[65] Michael Coveney, *The Financial Times* (London, the one printed on pink newsprint).

[66] *Spring Awakening*, 1984, Anne Bogart's interpretation of Frank Wedekind's 1891 work about teenage sexuality, with music of Leiber and Stoller, New York University Tisch School of the Arts, New York.

[67] *The Daily News*, December 13, 1984.

[68] Commentator Daniel Schorr on the subject of media coverage in national court cases (the O.J. Simpson trial, specifically), *All Things Considered*, National Public Radio, October 5, 1994.

[69] *The Village Voice,* March 29, 1988.

[70] *1951*, 1986, Anne Bogart with Mac Wellman, University of California/San Diego at the Mandell Weiss Center, La Jolla, then (1987), New York Theatre Workshop.

[71] *Orestes*, 1992, Charles L. Mee Jr., staged by Anne Bogart, Saratoga International Theater Institute.

[72] Just checking to see if you're paying attention. Matisse, in 1951, finished the Vence Chapel. He didn't die until 1954.

[73] "Much Ado About Adrian Hall," *TheaterWeek* magazine, July 20-26, 1992, Anderson.

[74] These and more figures were published in TCG's *American Theatre* magazine, "Theatre Facts," April 1994, and summarized in *The Village Voice*, April 26, 1994, the Teasers and Tormentors theater column, Anderson.

[75] *American Theatre,* April 1994.

[76] *SubUrbia*, by Eric Bogosian, opened in April 1994, at Lincoln Center's Mitzi E. Newhouse Theater in New York.

[77] Unpublished interview, Anderson, previously cited.

78 *The Medium,* 1993, previously cited.

79 At the time this commentary was prepared, Anne Bogart was scheduled to stage *The Adding Machine* as a part of the Actors Theatre of Louisville's 1995 Classics in Context festival, for which these comments were written.

80 *The Village Voice*, interview with Don Shewey, previously cited.

81 *Small Lives/Big Dreams*, previously cited.

82 *The Who's Tommy*, which might also be called "Springtime for Peter Townshend," revived the heaving old rock opera about the autistic-cum-messianic "pinball wizard" in such a way that it came closer than anything except, maybe, *Starlight Express*, to putting an MTV-style rock video into a live-stage format. With flown actors, an entirely fluid, lighting-installed set and frantic pace—not to mention a complete botching of the original's ending—the show opened April 22, 1993, at Broadway's St. James Theatre, a production of Jujamcyn Theatres with support from the touring-theater dynasty PACE Theatricals and the direction of Des McAnuff. *Tommy* revealed, maybe better than anything else to that date, what a lie it is to assert that giving young people theater that might speak to them stylistically will woo them back to the live art: Try taking a teen to *Tommy*, then to some Tennessee Williams. "Where are the lasers?" is the first petulant question you'll get, about three scenes into the Williams. *Tommy* is capitulation to and exploitation of techno-sensibility, not a subjugation of it to the needs of theater. At this writing, *Tommy* is still on Broadway playing to huge houses. Of course.

83 Erik Ehn, playwright, from an open letter to his Art Workers' Hostel/Assembly of the Wondrous Head, a group of small theaters trying to develop a national circuit of show exchanges, July 17, 1994. Ehn is based at Berkeley Rep in California.

84 *The Village Voice*, August 30, 1994, the Teasers and Tormentors theater column, Anderson.

85 *Small Lives/Big Dreams,* previously cited.

86 *Spin*, November 1994, Phillips Media's Magnavox 450 CD-i *Burn:Cycle*—the ad goes on to tempt you with this scenario (the "ticks" are included in the text): "Click forward to the year 2063 [tick] where

you've become a jaded [tick] nihilistic data thief named Sol Cutter [tick]
with a neural implant jack in your neck [tick] and one day while down-
loading corporate secrets [tick] into the software inside your skull [tick]
you also contract a nasty little [tick] computer virus called *Burn:Cycle*
[tick] which is basically gonna corrode your brain [tick] like battery
acid in two hours unless you can [tick] outwit and outshoot relentless
enemy agents [tick] find Doc the only guy who may know how to save
you [tick] then make peace with your personal demons [tick] and
somehow God help you [tick] locate the party responsible [tick] in this
cold harsh neon-lit world [tick] before you bite the oh what a bummer
[tick] your time's up." And that, unfortunately, is precisely the message
this game and its electronically, exponentially multiplying counterparts
might have for the art of live theater: Your time's up.

87 Erik Ehn, previously cited.

88 *The Medium,* previously cited.

◆    ◆    ◆

# Worlds of Bogart

by Mel Gussow

MEL GUSSOW IS A LONGTIME DRAMA CRITIC FOR *THE NEW York Times* and a winner of the George Jean Nathan Award for Dramatic Criticism. He has written profiles for *The New Yorker* and articles for other national magazines. The author of *Conversations with Pinter* and *Don't Say Yes Until I Finish Talking: A Biography of Darryl F. Zanuck,* and the recipient of a Guggenheim Fellowship, he is a past president of the New York Drama Critics Circle.

PANELIST

*Under the Influence:*
*Anne Bogart's Impact on Collaborators and Critics*

Actors Theatre of Louisville
Modern Masters—Anne Bogart

P eter Brook firmly believes in "unfreezing tradition." For him, the essence of theatre is "within a mystery called 'the present moment.'" In common with Brook, who stands as a sentinel to all theatrical experimentalists, Anne Bogart is a director of the present moment and, one might add, a director of the prescient moment. Relentlessly she searches for imaginative ways to renew the theatrical experience, to make it more relevant for herself and to those who are receiving it.

There are, of course, dangers inherent in such a procedure. In search of newness, a director can overlook the original impetus for a work of art and thereby negate its essential nature. Bogart tries to understand the reasons for a classic, asking why it was written, why it is considered to be a classic and why anyone should need to see it again. She is not a revisionist so much as a re-envisionist, an investigator probing the pulse of a work of dramatic art.

◆

She is certainly not alone in this endeavor. Peter Stein, Giorgio Strehler, Robert Wilson, Deborah Warner, Declan Donnellan, as well as Brook himself are all explorers on this path, and it is through their efforts that some of the most exciting contemporary theatre is being transmitted. One of Bogart's distinctions is her Americanness, her knowledge of our native idiom and what she refers to as our "gestural vocabulary," the body language that links people and that also separates them.

When she approaches American plays of the recent past, she regards them as "time capsules, memory capsules of who we are." To get to the source of the memory, she sweeps away cultural detritus. The more it is encrusted, the more she has to find a radical solution. The Rodgers and Hammerstein musical *South Pacific* may be the ultimate romanticization of World War II. When she staged the show early in her career, she filtered it through her memory of the wars that followed it, including the brief skirmish in Grenada. Under scrutiny were the different values justifying—or not justifying—those wars. Her *South Pacific* became a musical within a play set in an institution for emotionally disturbed veterans: it was a shellshocked *South Pacific*. The apparent inversion allowed her to comment on warfare, male bonding and the therapeutic effects of theatre itself. One would fully expect that if she had gone on to investigate *The King and I*, it would have dealt with the decline of colonialism. Whistle a happy tune as the sun sets on the empire.

◆

Many of her peers continue to do their work in small, confined venues, offering chamber plays to devoted partisans. These artists seem to thrive in isolation from the general public. Bogart has the potential to reach a wider audience and to influence mainstream theatre of her time. It might be said that her *South Pacific* foreshadowed the current trend of reimagining American musicals, as exemplified by Nicholas Hytner's production of *Carousel* and Harold Prince's production of *Show Boat*. Both of them tried to look beneath the surface and illuminate the social and psychological implications of these popular entertainments. Not many musicals and plays can stand such analysis.

Often considered an iconoclast, Bogart is actually a covert iconodulist, a venerator of images. But she is extremely careful about which images she chooses to venerate and how she chooses to express her attitude. Bogart brings to her work a sense of appreciation and a feeling of theatrical history. With plays that were first performed before her time, she is well aware of the initial circumstances and the associations that theatregoers have with the plays. She asks, "If you're doing *A Streetcar Named Desire*, do you pretend that Marlon Brando never played Stanley?" In her production of the play, the solution was to have 8 Stanleys and 12 Blanches, one of whom was a man. Though this was certainly an extreme measure, the motive was to shatter preconceptions and to encompass the world around *Streetcar*.

Up to now, she has specialized in four disparate areas of theatre:

- PERFORMANCE ART THAT REFLECTS OUR CULTURAL PAST. In this area, she is at her most collaborative. Playwrights write texts and, with the help of the actors, productions evolve, beginning with her trilogy about silent movies, vaudeville and marathon dancing, which she sees as landmarks of national identity.

- NEW APPROACHES TO FAMILIAR PLAYS, POPULAR AS WELL AS CLASSIC. Reaching into America's recent past, she has applied her skills to *Picnic, Once in a Lifetime* and *The Women* (and *South Pacific*), plays that in varying degrees might benefit from reassessment. With classics, she can find herself on less secure ground. Her version of Gorky's *Summerfolk* not only dismissed the samovars from the stage, it undercut the desperate longings of the characters. In contrast, the *Baal* that Robert Woodruff directed for her at Trinity Repertory Company bore the earmarks of the best of Bogart: insinuations of modernity without obscuring the ironic core of the work. Brecht's *Baal* became a burnout before he proved his creativity, a tragic story of artistic bankruptcy.

- FIRST PRODUCTIONS OF NEW PLAYS, AS EXEMPLIFIED BY EDUARDO MACHADO'S *IN THE EYE OF THE HURRICANE* AND PAULA VOGEL'S *THE BALTIMORE WALTZ*. Presented at the Actors Theatre of Louisville, her production of Machado's play sizzled with sudden changes of tempo and outlandish humor. Together the playwright and director orchestrated a dramatic tango about a self-disposable society in Cuba.

- BOGART BIODRAMAS, THEATRICAL PROFILES OF SIGNIFICANT PEOPLE. Although she has a full set of accomplishments in each of the four categories, it is in the last that she is making her most innovative contribution. The arc curves from her evening of Brecht's nondramatic writings to her evening of Marshall McLuhan's dramatic expostulations. The Brecht had a fully explanatory title, *No Plays No Poetry But Philosophical Reflections Practical Instructions Provocative Prescriptions Opinions and Pointers from a Noted Critic and Playwright*. The play, or environmental event, offered a comprehensive view of the playwright and his thought processes while also acting as a piece of Brechtian criticism.

◆

Walking into the theatre for *No Plays No Poetry* was like entering a theme park, *Verfremdungseffekwelt* (Alienation World). One was confronted by a sideshow barker spouting the author's aphorisms and antagonisms, and badgering the audience into finding a route on this seemingly unstructured journey. As it turned out, every stop was a sounding board. One came out of *No Plays No Poetry* with a more acute knowledge of Brecht's thoughts about the politics of theatre and the theatre of politics. In its indirect way, this original piece was Brechtian.

◆

Next to Brecht, McLuhan seems—or rather, should seem—untimely and even inconsequential, an artifact of the 1950s and possibly even a figure of fun. In Bogart's *The Medium*, McLuhan's message is reinstated. As a prophet, he becomes a doomsayer, a Canadian Cassandra foreseeing a Global Village controlled by computers. Is the information highway an organic extension of McLuhanism? In terms of style, the play is a kind of new vaudeville. Everything, including the actors, are at a tilt, as if they are wearing clownish "lean shoes." On an angular, highly physicalized landscape, actors move stiff-legged like characters in a Nuremberg clock. In this conception, McLuhan regains an air of mystery. As played by Tom Nelis, he looks a bit like that Hollywood mystery man Howard Hughes. And wouldn't Hughes be a fascinating subject for a future Bogart biodrama?

Taking off from a statement by Friedrich Duerrenmatt, Bogart maps the dimensions of her theatre. If you go to the theatre and put your hands over your eyes and still understand what is happening onstage, then the play is a lecture. If you put your hands over your ears and still understand what is happening, then it is a slide lecture. It is her credo that theatre begins when there is tension between the action and the word, choreography and psychology. In her world, opposites collide and theatre provokes all our senses.

◆

It was once said about her that she is "a stylish, versatile, thoughtful impresario...she has managed in a relatively brief but wide-ranging career to mix serious thoughts with wild imagination, profane with the sacred, humor with messages, and laughter with despair." That was written in an editorial in *The Providence Journal*, welcoming her to Providence as the new artistic director of the Trinity Repertory Company. Although she proved to be too adventurous for Trinity, the truth of that statement remains.

◆  ◆  ◆

# The Paradox of the Circle: Anne Bogart's Creative Encounter with East Asian Performance Traditions

by Eelka Lampe

EELKA LAMPE IS A NEW YORK-BASED WRITER WHO HAS also collaborated as a dramaturg and director in Germany, France and the United States. She received her Ph.D. from New York University and is currently working on a book about Anne Bogart. Her essays on performing artist Rachel Rosenthal, director Linda Mussmann and Ms. Bogart have been published in *The Drama Review, Women and Performance,* and a recent anthology entitled *Acting [Re]Considered.*

Avant-garde theatre director Anne Bogart has made a name for herself in the U.S. theatre community through her deconstructions of modern classics such as the musical *South Pacific* (1984), *Cinderella/Cendrillon* (1988) after Massenet's opera, Büchner's *Danton's Death* (1986), Gorki's *Summerfolk* (1989), Inge's *Picnic* (1992), as well as through her idiosyncratic original dance/theatre "compositions" she develops collaboratively with her respective ensemble. Prominent compositions were *1951* (1986) on art and politics during the McCarthy era, *No Plays No Poetry* (1988) on Brecht's theoretical writings, *American Vaudeville* (1991), and *The Medium* (1993) on McLuhan's writings. Furthermore, Bogart has been acclaimed for her astute directing of the work by contemporary playwrights, such as Paula Vogel, Charles Mee, Jr. and Eduardo Machado.

In the current lingo of theatre criticism and academia Bogart's deconstructionist approaches to directing can easily be labeled as postmodern. For example, her concept for *South Pacific* was that it took place in a rehab clinic for war veterans who had to relearn American society's (gender) rituals. Furthermore, Bogart's insistence on nonrealistic dissociative acting styles supports her placement in the arena of postmodern directors. In her disruptions of conventional acting the modern coherent subject gets split up in multiple selves who interact with each other on kinesthetic rather than psychological grounds. For instance, Cinderella had her alter ego in *Cendrillon*, Lillian Hellman in *1951* was split up in an "objective" and a "subjective" one, Danton in Büchner's revolutionary drama found his identity multiplied by numerous "Danton's Textual Counterparts." However, through many years of immersing myself into Bogart's work (I began watching my first rehearsals in 1984), I consider such labeling as quite limiting.

For me the key to an understanding of Bogart's work on a deeper level lies in looking at her longterm interaction with East Asian performance aesthetics and philosophy. Bogart's thorough ongoing involvement with traditional Chinese and Japanese performance practice and theory has led her to challenge the acting dogma of American psychological realism with the longterm goal to revamp the American theatre from the inside out. Paradoxically, Bogart embarked on this path to (re)discover theatre in its, what she sometimes calls, real American form: "I only grow when I encounter other cultures. It challenges me to understand my own better. I want to do very American art" (Bogart 1994).

◆

Bogart's directing has been influenced by the philosophy and practice of Chinese and Japanese martial arts (Tai Chi Chuan and Aikido) from the onset of her career in the mid 1970s. She became a practitioner of Tai Chi Chuan in 1974 and began in the early '80s with Aikido, which is more combat-oriented but utilizes the same interactive axioms as Tai Chi Chuan. The impact of these forms on her directing is subtle but all-pervasive.

Tai Chi, which is based on the philosophy of taosim, has given her conceptual support and inspiration for a nonautocratic way of directing. Principles like noninterference, being open to what the other has to offer, and letting go of the restrictive investments of the self have allowed Bogart to develop a collaborative, i.e. nonhierarchical, kinesthetic composition technique which she calls "Viewpoints," alluding to improvisational explorations in postmodern dance from which she got the structural ideas for her own categories. Bogart's currently nine Viewpoints are spatial relationship, shape, kinesthetic response, gesture, repetition, architecture, tempo, duration, and topography. By using this composition technique to train her performers and to ultimately let them create what she calls an "external tapestry" on stage, Bogart delegates major creative responsibility to her performers regarding the scenic composition of her mise-en-scènes.

To direct this way takes strength. It requires Bogart to let go of the traditional directorial ego. Such allowing of forces other than one's own mind to determine the aesthetics of a piece partakes in taoist ideas: to be grounded in a stillness which allows for a deep responsiveness to the world around oneself. From a Western perspective, I see Bogart working with what de Lauretis in *Technologies of Gender* (1987) calls a "feminist subjectivity:" Bogart is affirming her own gendered subject position as a director but from that patriarchically inherited position of directorial power, she renegotiates the traditional directorial role. Her deliberate act of giving up control during the creative process becomes a political act, in this context, a feminist response to conventional hierarchical structures. I define Bogart's practice at this intersection of taoism and feminism as an example of a "feminist subjectivity centered but egoless."

Beyond the Asian influence in the practical manifestations of her directing philosophy, Bogart borrows East Asian concepts for her stage language. These include "physical state," concentrating on the center, "less face," as well as movement principles like yielding and circular patterns of interaction. With her movement-oriented way of working, she challenges actors to create a physical score that exists independently from the verbal expression of their characters. Through this "technique of dissociation" which I have written about elsewhere (Lampe 1992), Bogart disrupts Western representational conventions which support a cultural status quo by, for example, replicating the performance of gender hierarchy in the verbal and physical codes of psychological realism. As an example, in *The Medium*, Tom Nelis playing Marshall McLuhan was going through stylized convulsions while lecturing on the effects of mass media on human relationships. In this case, a male-gendered authoritative body language which customarily accompanies the representation of Western discourse was disrupted and thereby parodied.

In September 1994 at a post-show discussion of *Small Lives/Big Dreams*, in which five characters personify the essence of Chekhov's five major plays, Bogart responded to the question of what role voice/language plays in her seemingly so dance-oriented theatre. "We were just talking about that this summer. And Bondo (actor Will Bond) said: 'Voice should be the last thing—the poetry—when there is nothing else left to do.' Now that idea is totally different from American realism where voice/language is always the first and most important thing."[1]

Actress Karenjune Sánchez commented on the connection between the precise choreography and the verbal emotional expression when working with Bogart: "It has to be so precisely choreographed so that whom we're talking to can change each night." Only because every movement is precisely set, the actors are free to feel differently and therefore respond differently to one another in every single performance.

The notion of freedom inside the form is a fundamental principle of East Asian aesthetics which martial arts share with performance traditions, such as Beijing Opera or Japanese Noh. Bogart has adapted this and other East Asian performance principles to inform her Western, and as I see it, feminist directing practice. Instead of "orientalizing" Asian performance traditions (see Said 1978) to strengthen the identity of Western culture, Bogart has distilled a few principles from those traditions (and "abused" them in an irreverent alliance with a feminist critique of representation) in order to question the identity of Western culture.

Bogart believes that Western theatre, or more precisely, the American branch of Western theatre which perpetuates psychological realism and therefore a status quo in the power fabrics of social relationships, is in a state of crisis. According to her, the dominant acting style based on Strasberg's Method is hopelessly outdated, i.e. it still works for TV and film [as mainstream media perhaps more prone to hegemonic practices?] but not anymore for theatre "if theatre wants be taken seriously as an art form." Although Bogart participates here somewhat nebulously in a discourse of searching for "true art," another implication can be read into her statement: Theatre where it is not commercial has the status of a fringe medium and from that vantage point it has a different potential for a critique of Representation writ large.

Bogart focuses on principles instead of the outer exhibitionistic shell of Asian theatre. This is in itself quite true to the priorities in Asian performance cultures. Bogart's main source of inspiration has been Tai Chi which as a martial arts form does not so easily lend itself to a misrepresentation of the worst kind of Orientalism which I would call "Ornamentalism." At its root, Tai Chi is not about performing (for others), it is in the doing (for oneself), for meditating, for health, for self-defense. Any serious practitioner will continuously be looking for a clean execution of the principles; the external appearance is less important, or rather, will fall into place if the principles are being carefully observed. In my observation, Bogart has adapted this kind of thinking for her directing: The interior physical principles have to be clean and clear, and that implies they have to be true to the individual performer; then the rest, i.e. the exterior expression, will simply fall into place.

A logical extension of Bogart's interests beneath the surface of "Ornamentalism" is her recent cofounding of Saratoga International Theater Institute (SITI) with Japanese avant-garde director Tadashi Suzuki. Begun in 1992 and envisioned as an alternative to the ailing regional theatre, SITI wants to support and feature multicultural expression in the theatre through productions, workshops, and symposia. This grand multicultural vision I find rather problematic at this stage of their organizational and artistic development. So far only bilingual productions directed by Suzuki with mixed Japanese and American casts and productions by Bogart with primarily American actors have been presented. Furthermore, the symposia consisted of only white American artists and scholars, Suzuki himself being the exception. In other words, at this point in time (September 1994), "bicultural" exchange seems a more adequate label for the reality of SITI. Inherent in this critique is also the observation that with an American/Japanese leadership team there is the danger of perpetuating a "first world" hegemony in relationship to other future collaborators. But it is premature to fabricate a further critique of a young organization before their longterm multicultural goals have even been put into practice.

◆

For the purpose of the current discussion, I want to focus on the real discernible effects of the Bogart-Suzuki collaboration with my main attention on Bogart's work. Similar to Bogart's search for principles, Suzuki has essentialized theatrical axioms from Japanese classical performing traditions for his avant-garde renditions of Western classics, such as *Dionysus* from *The Bacchae* or *Tale of Lear* from *King Lear.* What happens to Bogart's vision and search through this connection? Bogart absorbs and transforms. Concretely, Suzuki-trained American performers flourish in her Viewpoints improvisations. As Bogart explained at their lecture demonstration in Saratoga Springs on September 24, 1994, the Suzuki Method is about facing and checking oneself every day, and the Viewpoints are about facing one another. There is an interesting correspondence here to Tai Chi Chuan, where the solo exercise is about working on "the self," i.e. developing one's internal energy, and "push hands," the martial arts practice, is about responding to somebody else's energy. The Suzuki-trained performers' extraordinary capabilities for physical expression, which is focussed and rooted from the waist down (and not psychologically motivated), serve as a perfect technical foundation for Bogart who then directs her performers to juxtapose their collectively created Viewpoints movement scores with the verbal text and thus evoke the tension and therefore the disruption in representation that she is looking for.

Despite my initial caution with regard to labeling, both Suzuki and Bogart in their pastiche approaches are postmodern directors. Suzuki, however, is still "modern" in his search for one man's vision (his own). Moreover, he demands unity of expression: The "animal energy" that he hopes to trigger in his performers through his rigorous training can ideally only release an integrated expression of verbal and body language. Bogart, in contrast, irreverently questions this connection, not as one that can still be found in human reality, but as one that is enlightening for the artistic medium of theatre in the late 20th century. She is not interested in an organic "animal energy" but in the alienation of conventional behavior confronting the spectator's eye—a very Brechtian impulse at its core.

Anne Bogart chose to venture toward the Far East to search for different "truths," i.e. physical principles, of human expression rather than what Western acting craft could offer her. She is certainly not alone in this journey. Meyerhold, Brecht, Grotowski, and Barba looked East long before her, and many other theatre and dance artists have done so before and since. But

Bogart is not interested in romanticizing "the East," which I contend Grotowski and Barba are still doing in their different pursuits of an ultimate organic intercultural acting expression. For her, it has been a search for tools to strengthen her own ulterior motive—to critique the model of theatre as the mirror of (Western patriarchal) culture. In her mise-en-scènes, Bogart smashes the mirror and confronts people with her ensemble's eruptive mosaic of the contradictions of Western civilization.

But ironically, after reaching out to the East, Bogart has more recently found herself circling back "home." Paradoxically, through her encounter with Suzuki and his essentializing of Japanese performative heritage, Bogart desired more and more to unearth American "roots"[2] which could provide her with comparable food for creation. In this endeavor, Bogart stumbled upon Martha Graham as a potential American source for her own theatrical drive against psychological realism.

◆

In *Chronicles of Tao* (1993), a historical biographical novel about a Taoist monk and martial artist, a Taoist master tells his disciple that "on the extreme limits of knowledge" one finds paradox which should not be confused with contradiction. Whereas paradox stands for the simultaneous existence of opposing qualities in a thing or a situation, contradiction is an exclusionary, irreconcilable opposition. I conceive of Bogart's encounter with East Asian performing traditions as the paradox of the circle. By that I mean the movement of any circle is an opening up in order to close itself and that is a perpetual motion. Bogart has been opening herself up to Eastern traditions in order to come full circle, back to a deeper digging into and understanding of her own cultural background. I am convinced that this circular journey won't be the last one that Bogart undertakes. Talking about her Viewpoints recently, Bogart elaborated, "It's a philosophy of movement. It's about not stopping things."Looking at circular motion as open-ended, as one that only pretends to represent closure, where ongoing means uncovering deeper layers of the same rather than discovering higher realms of the other—these are some reflections that for me reverberate Bogart's encounter with East Asian performance traditions. Bogart's martial arts practice and her collaboration with Suzuki-trained performers is simply and quietly an ongoing learning experience, an enrichment through the negotiation of difference.

◆    ◆    ◆

# Annotations

[1] The dissociation of dialogue became a complex issue in *Small Lives/Big Dreams*. Karenjune Sánchez, for example, portrayed her personalized essence of *Three Sisters*. In baggy grey clown's pants held by suspenders, she occasionally physically evoked vaudeville routines, like balancing a tea cup on her bowler hat. Yet, while doing so, she stubbornly and angrily screamed, "I am sooo happy!" During this, the *Uncle Vanja* and the *Cherry Orchard* characters seriously puzzled or mused over their upside down tea cups on saucers. This is an instance where the re-presentation of language emerged as critical distortion of realistic dialogue. But simultaneously language became sculpture, sparse but significant, and yet, ultimately, only one additional fleeting "viewpoint" to counterbalance the overall composition. This stands in sharp contrast to the usual dominance in Western theatre of language over the other channels of communication.

[2] Bogart's journey Eastward threw her into a personal crisis to come to terms with her own American heritage, and that process is still under way. The elusiveness and loadedness of the term "heritage," its historical construction, and the recurrent desire in diverse cultural politics to pinpoint "origins" of "authentic" cultural expression West or East alike is a rich topic for another essay. For Bogart the theatre artist the search is real and crucial. Whether the question of heritage or origin can be deconstructed as ultimately unreal is totally beside the point for a director whose existential and artistic survival is based on deconstructing and reassembling cultural constructions of the past and the present.

◆　　◆　　◆

# References

Bogart, Anne (1994) Comments at a lecture/demonstration on the Suzuki Method and Bogart's Viewpoints at Saratoga International Theater Institute, Saratoga Springs, NY.

de Lauretis, Teresa (1987) *Technologies of Gender*. Bloomington and Indianapolis: University of Indiana Press.

Deng, Ming-Dao (1993) *Chronicles of Tao: The Secret Life of a Taoist Master*. New York: HarperCollins.

Lampe, Eelka (1992) "From the Battle to the Gift: The Directing of Anne Bogart." *TDR* 36, no.1 (T133):14-47.

Said, Edward (1978) *Orientalism*. New York: Random House.

# ◆ PERFORMANCE TEXT ◆

# Small Lives/Big Dreams:
## Adapted from the Five Major
## Plays of Anton Chekhov

conceived by Anne Bogart
and created by the SITI Company

◆

SPECIAL NOTE: Simultaneous dialogue is designated by text that is preceded by an * or text that is in smaller type and indented.

# PROLOGUE

A stone is thrown onto the stage followed by a little girl in a red nightgown. As she plays with the stone, two other figures appear—a woman carrying a parasol and a man holding a teacup. It is a lovely early morning. As the child plays, a low rumble is heard, then the sound of an earthquake. Walls shake, sirens wail, glass breaks and the city crumbles to the ground. Women and men run about pulling each other from burning buildings. Some collapse to the ground dead, some run for their lives. Finally a lone man is left on stage. He is badly shocked and cerebrally damaged. As he attempts to walk off, he is caught off-guard by his own short physical spasms.

# MOVEMENT ONE

A road. A woman, **CO**, in torn white Victorian clothing appears, holding her shoes in her hands. She is heading down the road. Walking down this road clearly requires an effort of will. She has the attitude of someone who normally knows where she is going but in this case there is no normality. She is doing the best she can. She, too, has been damaged. Her home is gone and all she knows is to move forward into an uncertain future. She can barely remember who she is. She is followed by a girl, **UV**, in red who crawls rather than walks. Then a man, **I**, carrying a teacup delicately balanced on a bulky suitcase. He carries many awkward remnants of his old life. He is followed by a man, **TS**, trotting steadily along the road in bare feet, reading a book. The last figure to cross the stage, **S**, is the man who was earlier shaken by spasms. His head is bandaged. He carries a birdcage and a walking stick which he digs with determination into the ground as he travels down the road. All five characters disappear down the road.

Further along, a bowler hat lands on the road. **CO** follows, carrying a white parasol. One by one the others appear behind her, all struggling to continue their journey. Having lost their facility with speech, they speak in aphasic fragments. The sounds of the words are hollow and disjointed, as if each were calling into a well.

**TS**   A quarter past eight—

**I**   Please.

**CO**   (*Singing.*) *What is this noisy world to me?*
*Oh, what are friends and foes?*
*Oh, that my heart were cheered*
*By the warmth of requited love!*
Horrible the way these people sing.

**TS**   I don't know.
I don't know.
Tea would be nice.

**UV**   Say a prayer—

**S**   Haven't had any experiences, confound it all.

**I**   Surprise!

**S**   That's all there is to it.
My leg's—gone.

**CO**   Every day I repeat—oh!

**I**   A cry from the heart.

**TS**   What a noise!

**CO**   I keep expecting something to happen

**UV**   Here you have my life and...

**TS**   There's more light

**UV**   I don't know what—

| | |
|---|---|
| **CO** | Is that—music? |
| **TS** | Someone's coming. |
| **S** | Amazing! |
| **UV** | Thoughts—ah— |
| **TS** | Hello. |
| **I** | Done with a purpose. |
| **CO** | We are going to bypass all the petty illusions that keep people from being happy and free—that's the goal of our life, its meaning.<br>Forward then. |
| **TS** | I'm tired. |
| **CO** | We are advancing toward that bright star glowing in the distance. |
| **TS** | I'm tired. |
| **CO** | Nothing can hold us back.<br>Forward march! |
| **TS** | I want some tea. |
| **CO** | Don't lag behind.<br>To live in the present we first have to make up for our past, to have done with it once and for all.<br>Be as free as the wind.<br>Marvelous visions of the future.<br>I can already see it...<br>The moon is rising! |
| **UV** | Illusions— |
| **TS** | Actual time doesn't matter. |

**S**       Next thing I'll do is—

**I**       To go home again

**TS**     Purpose—

**CO**    And if we are not meant to see it, if we are not to know it, what does that matter—

**TS**     I know so little, oh, so little!

**S**       Women!

**TS**     Obvious we don't understand one another.

**S**       If you only knew how—

**I**       I have got somehow transformed into a sort of Hamlet or Manfred.

**S**       What's there to understand?

**TS**     Cranes for example.

**S**       What's there to understand?

**CO**    Ladies and gentlemen—the sun has set. (*Starts to move off, continuing down the road.*)

**TS**     They'll go on flying.
A meaning...
Look, it's snowing!

**S**       The devil take it.
The devil take my vanity—sucks out my blood, sucks it out like a—

**I**       This is no place.

**UV**    I'm not... beautiful— (*Exits, following **CO**.*)

**TS**   What a wind! (*Exits, tossing his hat ahead of him.*)

**S**   You've heard of obsessions, when a man is haunted by the idea of the moon or something? Well, I've got my moon.

**I**   Go away, go! (*Exits.*)

**S**   Same old tune.
Fraud!
Who am I—Agamemnon?
All over again, from the beginning.
I don't feel like leaving.
I don't really feel like leaving—
A subject flashed through my head.

(*He rushes off suddenly and disappears.*)

# MOVEMENT TWO

Further down the road, **CO** appears again, carrying her parasol and a picnic basket. She is followed by the others. They begin to speak in a fugue-like manner, occasionally overlapping. Unaccustomed to the sounds they are uttering, they chisel their words to sculpt newly found sentences. Words become depth sounders sent out in search of one another. They set up a roadside camp. In an attempt to reconstruct their lives, they hold a tea party and put on a play.

**TS**   I thought I would never live through it.

**CO**   What time is it? It's light already.

**UV**   How many years—

**CO**   I thought you had gone. I slept through it.

**UV**   Lord help—

**TS**     You were in a dead faint, as though you were dead.

**CO**    Went dead to sleep sitting up. If only you might've awakened me.

**TS**     And the clock was striking...I remember.

**CO**    I remember when I was fifteen...

**UV**    Gone–changed then? I have–different person.

**I**      It's hot!

**CO**    My father punched me in the face with his fist. I remember it as if it were today.

**TS**     It was raining.

**CO**    A bull in a china shop.

**TS**     I don't want to think about it.
> **UV**    From morning until night I am always–

**UV**    Not a moment's... Music!... I lie in continual. Life itself– dirty. Life swallows–I might play! Drags you–like this. Little–you become strange–never notice–

**CO**    Here's this book that I was reading without any attention and fell asleep.

**UV**    I've turned into–queer fish.

**TS**     I remember perfectly. As if it were yesterday. When I woke this
> **I**    You won't believe me, but I've covered fif-teen miles in less

morning, I saw the spring light. My soul responded to that light, and
> than three hours. I'm worn out. Just feel my heart. See how it's thumping.

I wanted so much to go back home.
             Do you hear? Tum–tum–tum–tum–tum.
Don't whistle. *Please*. How can you.

(*S enters abruptly, banging his walking stick on the ground. All turn to stare at him. The pace quickens.*)

**CO**    What's the matter with you? You're all...

**S**     I mourn for my lost life. I am unhappy.

**CO**    My hands are shaking. I'm going to faint.

**I**     I might die.

**UV**    Brains–feelings–dead to the world.

**TS**    My head is splitting. Strange thoughts come to me.

**S**     Why?

***I***    Tell me, will you be sorry if I die? This is positively un-
          bearable. I wish you'd understand how maddening it is.
***CO***   Better remember who you are. I am tired of you. I am
          used to it. I must be going.
***TS***   I have been feeling as if every day had been drained
          from me. And only one thought in my heart. To go
          away. Leave all and go. As soon as possible.
***UV***   Nothing–nothing–nothing–nothing–nothing–

**S**     I don't understand.

**UV**    Something to eat.
             **CO**    There I go again...

**CO**    Pardon the expression, but accidents like these...they're
          simply phenomenal.

(*Suddenly, this accumulation of activity and speaking
stops. They look at each other uneasily. After a*

*moment of discomfort and disorientation, the follow-*
*ing occurs in stillness, as if suspended in time.)*

**S**      I guess something is going to happen here soon.

**UV**      Weren't wanted—feelings—wake up.

**TS**      The main thing in life is form—when things lose their form, they lose their identity.

**CO**      When he talks, one doesn't know what he means. It doesn't make sense.

**S**      It's too late to change my ways.

**CO**      What's wrong with me? I'm shivering all over.

**I**      What's the use of discussing things with people like you?

**TS**      He doesn't live on food like the rest of us. He lives on philosophy.

**I**      You and I, brother, are past the age of thinking about a philosophy of life.

**S**      I have to hurry. I can't stay. I just can't.

**CO**      It must be time to go.

*(They jerk into action again, attempting to continue with the tasks at hand.)*

**UV**      Sat down. Sat down, shut eyes—just this, think. People live a

> **CO**    Will she recognize me, I wonder? Will she know me again,

hundred—two—struggling now—the way—a road—remember?

wonder? I am going to faint... I am going to faint.

People will not—our life knocked.

**I**    Why are you stamping around like that? Leave me alone please!

**TS**    I suddenly felt glad and remembered my childhood.

(*A bell rings. They move into a fugue state.*)

**TS**    And such *thoughts* moving me. Such wonderful thoughts—such *memories*...

**UV**    The bell!

**TS**    And what a happy life I dreamed of then.

**I**    Let's go and do somersaults.

**CO**    I am like a little girl again. Can you believe it?

**TS**    Today I'm free. I haven't got a headache, and I feel younger than I was yesterday. All's well, God is everywhere.

**CO**    My dog eats nuts.

**S**    This morning I woke up with a splitting headache. As if my brain were glued to my skull. And I unexpectedly fell asleep again, and now all my bones ache and I can hardly breathe. I'm a complete wreck, my life's a nightmare.

**I**    What a memory!

**TS**    I'm sick of listening to you. He likes to hear himself talk. I would have left long ago.

**CO**    At last you've come.

**I**        I'm going to have a swim and chew some paper.

**S**        That dog will howl all night again.

**UV**        To be waked—sleep.

**TS**        I feel as if I were sailing, a broad blue sky above me, great white birds flying by. Why is that? Why? When I got up today it suddenly struck me that the world made sense. It was all clear to me—the way I had to live. I know it all. We must live by the sweat of our brow. That is the whole meaning of life. All happiness. All enthusiasm. Oh, it's awful!

        *(They look at each other again, uncomfortably try to reassess what just happened to them. Finally one is able to speak. Again they are suspended in the moment, unable to move.)*

**UV**        Don't worry.

**S**        I've nowhere to go, confound it all. Let's go.

**TS**        A new age is dawning.

**UV**        One or two—I must do.

**S**        What a mess!

**TS**        The time has come, a massive cloud is descending upon us, a powerful, invigorating storm is gathering. It's on its way, I feel it already.

**UV**        Hot!

**CO**        I'm frozen.

**TS**        You don't matter.

**CO**        I must tell you something. It cannot wait another moment.

**TS**     In twenty-five years you'll be dead—thank God.

**S**      Like it or not, you have to go on living.

           (*They jolt into action again, setting up the tea party.*)

**CO**     Now what? Same old story.

**UV**     I've never seen—more beautiful woman. Her eyes—
           exquisite
>                    **CO**     I don't know what to make of it. If only I
>                               could get to sleep.
           woman. One foot rummaging
>                               I didn't sleep the whole way, I was so anx-
>                               ious. I won't be a minute.
           books—dawn—new life.
>                               Thank god you've come.
           *The hut is cold, the fire is dead.*
           *Where shall the master lay his head?*

**S**      There is our theater! Absolutely no scenery! The audi-
           ence has an open view of the horizon. The moon rises.

**I**      I would stop talking nonsense if I were you. If only you
           could take a good smack at something, enough to make
           sparks fly, I mean.

**S**      It's the tragedy of my life. And all the rest of it.

**I**      You're a neurotic, a weakling. Take me, for instance.
           You see what I'm driving at? You don't do anything for
           yourself, and you won't let me do anything, either.

**UV**     Learned fish—complaining.

**S**      Oh, she's bored. She's jealous. She is a psychological
           curiosity.

**CO**     Don't tell me about it, don't...

**S**  We are all her enemies. It's all our fault. She's superstitious, afraid of the number thirteen, or three candles on a table.

**CO**  She has nothing left, nothing.

**UV**  Nothing about art. Wasting time.

**CO**  What's happening? Oh my God! My God!
What—What— He is absolutely unknown.

**TS**  He's up to something.

*(Suddenly CO hyperventilates and convulses as a real memory surfaces.)*

**CO**  Uha—Uha—Uha—Uha—

**S**  Calm down. You are nervous and the rest of it. Set your mind at rest.

**CO**  There's nothing to it. It's all a dream.

**I**  All this is just nonsense, nonsense, nonsense. Nonsense and pretense.

**TS**  How annoying.

**CO**  In Paris I flew in a balloon!

**UV**  Envious.

**TS**  My kingdom for a cup of tea.

**S**  Loves me—loves me not—loves me—loves me not!!

> **I**  Just look at him. Sour, depressed, gloomy, miserable.

She doesn't love me. Why should she? She wants to live, to love...

| CO | If I let you kiss my hand, it'll be my elbow next, then my shoulder. |
|---|---|

She knows I don't respect contemporary theater. She imagines

|   | What are we to do? |
|---|---|

she's serving humanity, the cause of sacred art. But as I see it,

| I | Come on, clever, show me the way to get ahead. There's nothing to show... |
|---|---|

our theater is in a rut—it's so damn conventional. The modern

|   | Useless people, useless talk. |
|---|---|

stage is nothing but an old prejudice, nothing but a sad and dreary routine. They strive to squeeze out a moral from the flat, vulgar pictures and the flat vulgar phrases, a little tiny moral, easy to comprehend and handy for home consumption. In a thousand variations they offer me always the same thing over and over again. I run and keep on running as fast as Maupassant ran from the brain-crushing vulgarity of the Eiffel Tower. But the stage is certainly an important factor in culture. We must have a new formula. That's what we want. And if there are none, then it's better to have nothing at all.

| CO | The birds are singing. |
|---|---|

| S | That depresses me. |
|---|---|

| TS | How odd... |
|---|---|

*(Once again, they are motionless, caught up in a suspension like an inhaled breath.)*

| CO | What time is it now? It must be past two. It must be time to go. |
|---|---|

| I | All this has tired me to the point of making me ill. I have a headache. I can't sleep. There are noises in my ears. There's simply nowhere where I can get any peace. |
|---|---|

**CO** What bliss!

**TS** It's as dead as the bottom of the sea.

**CO** One would hardly know you. How you've changed!
Who are you? Don't you remember? What now? I've lost
all my hairpins. *Yoohoo!* There I go again. I just knew it.

**UV** Her youth over.
Her beauty faded.
Man she loved dead.

**CO** I can't bring myself to believe it. Time flies.

**I** My mind's so confused.

**S** What could be more desperate and absurd than my position?

**I** I feel in the grip of a kind of indolence. I can't understand myself or other people.

**UV** Forgive—have changed. I hardly know—

**CO** You haven't changed a bit.

**S** In times gone by I had two great wishes. But I accom-
plished neither.

**I** I would like to tell you the whole story from the beginning. It's so long and complicated that I could hardly
hope to finish it. There's nothing remarkable about me. I
don't feel any love or pity but just a sort of indifference
and lassitude. The owl—it screeches every night.

**UV** I want to talk.

**TS** What *can* that mean? What *can* that mean?

**S** I am insanely happy.

**TS**   Don't cry.

**CO**   Can this really be me sitting here? I feel like dancing and waving my arms about. And what if it is a dream!

*(They lurch into action again, setting up a teaparty in the midst of their improvised campground.)*

**UV**   Shining personality I used to be. On purpose blind myself I
> **CO**   A young lady should never forget herself.

tried. Doing the I thought was right thing. Because of the can't sleep
> > There's nothing I dislike so much in a girl as loose behavior.

at night. How stupidly the anger disappointment I let glide by time.
> > I'd love to just stare at you a while, talk.

I could have had the years everything I wasted. Dreadful it. I'll hold my tongue. Fine day. Hot. Hang oneself. Chick, chick, chick. Speckled hen walked. Damned annoying that's like me. I have the honor to wish you all.

**CO**   You are magnificent, as always.

**TS**   What? I don't like this. What are you doing? You are shameless. I am glad. Very glad. I remember. I forget your faces. How time does fly! Oh, how time flies. Now I seem to remember your face. I don't remember you. I don't really remember you. You know, it is so *vague*, really, so vague. I can close my eyes and see him as he was. I used to think I remembered everybody, but... I remember. Do you remember? That's it. What a surprise! And I'm crying too. Nobody knows why. I know why. Because if it was near it wouldn't be far off, and if it's far off, it can't be near. Now I know who you are. I remember. I'm beginning to forget her face. We'll be forgotten in just the same way. Yes, they'll forget us. It's our fate, it can't be helped.

**CO**     He can say what he likes, I don't care.

**S**      I'm not late am I? No, no, no! There's a red glow in the sky, the moon is beginning to rise. But now I'm happy. See how difficult it is for me to breathe. I have to hurry. I can't stay, I just can't. My heart is full of you. We are alone. What sort of tree is that. Why is it is dark? It's evening already; everything looks darker. It's time to begin.

**CO**     I can't sit still! I can't do it! This happiness is more than I can bear. Laugh at me! I am a fool!

**S**      Are you nervous? I'm embarrassed.

*(Pandemonium erupts.)*

*\*TS*    Wasn't it thought that some rubbish written by a fool, held all the truth?

*\*CO*    I'm off in a moment, there's no time to talk.

*\*S*     One must depict life not as it is, nor as it should be, but as it appears in dreams.

*\*CO*    Well, I'll be brief. There's a way out. Listen to me carefully. I don't quite understand what you mean. Excuse me, but you don't know what you're talking about. Come on, make up your mind! Shut up!

*\*UV*    Nice this is all very. Convincing but it's not.

*\*I*     Maybe you can see through me. You don't like me, and you don't conceal it. I've only got to open my mouth and say one word. We're left here alone. It's a hideous existence.

*\*UV*    Only a thoughtless barbarian could burn beauty like this. We are endowed with reason and creative force to increase what has been given us; until now; we have not created but destroyed.

*\*CO*    They knew the way to do things then...And where are those ways now?

*\*S*     But you like to give me pain. (*Sings loudly*) *Never say youth is wasted.*

S   What do you want of me? *Be quiet!*

   (*Everyone stops, looking to the source of this outburst.*
   *S is triumphant.*)

S   The stage has gone to the dogs. There were mighty oaks,
   but now we see nothing but stumps. When does the
   thing begin?
      *O Hamlet, speak no more*
     *Thou turnst my eyes into my very soul,*
     *And there I see such black and grained spots*
      *As will not leave their tinct.*
       *Nay, but to live*
     *In the rank sweat of an enseamed bed.*
    *Stewed in corruption, honeying and making love*
      *Over the nasty sty—*
   We are about to begin!
   Attention please! (*Pause.*) I'll begin. (*He knocks three*
   *times on the ground and speaks in a loud voice.*) Ye
   venerable, hoary shadows, ye who hover o'er this ocean
   at night, I bid ye, sink us into a sleep and let us dream
   what will be in two hundred thousand years. In two
   hundred thousand years there will be nothing. Show us
   this nothing. For thousands of centuries the earth has
   borne no living creature, and this poor moon lights its
   lamp in vain. In the meadows cranes no longer awaken
   with a cry, May beetles are silent in the lindens. (*He*
   *shrieks at TS, who is sleeping.*)

TS   Cheep, cheep, cheep...

S   Empty, empty, empty. Terrible, terrible, terrible.
   The bodies of living creatures have turned to dust and all
   their souls have merged into one. I am that World Soul.
   In me there live the souls of Alexander, of Caesar, Shakespeare, Napoleon and also the soul of the smallest
   worm.

CO   What's he talking about?

**I**      I understand.

**S**      In me human consciousness has merged with animal instinct. I remember all, all, all, and every life that is within me I live through again. I open my lips to speak, and my voice echoes mournfully in the void, and no one hears.

**CO**      What's he talking about?

**S**      In the universe only spirit remains permanent and immutable. I don't know where I am and what awaits me. Only one truth has been revealed to me: I am destined to triumph. Then matter and spirit will fuse in glorious harmony, and the kingdom of universal freedom will come to pass. Till then, horror, horror.

**CO**      You talk too much.

**I**      I understand. You can tell me about your depression.

**CO**      I never lose hope.
I'll be thinking everything's gone down the drain, I'm sunk, and wham! You'll see something will turn up, if not today then tomorrow. The starlings are singing! You haven't forgotten? You remember, don't you? You haven't forgotten? Oh, my childhood, my innocent childhood! Happiness awoke with me every morning! It was just like this, nothing has changed. All, all white. After the dark, dismal autumn and the cold, cold winter you are young again, full of happiness. The angels of heaven have not abandoned you. Oh! If only I could free my neck and shoulders from the stone that weighs them down! If only I could forget my past. Look there she
      **UV**      She is in love—I understand—
is! There's no one really there, really. It only looked like it.

**TS**      We are very petty. See how little I am. All right, that's enough. I couldn't sleep all night. Shut my eyes.

Couldn't sleep. Everything racing through my mind. Nothing happened. Before I knew it, it was dawn.

CO      He never gives up.
Go away. You smell of chicken.

S      I don't mind listening to nonsense now and again for fun; but I see nothing but evil disposition.

CO      If only God would help us!

I      The owl's screeching again. You know, I'm beginning to think that Fate's cheated me. Lots of people who are probably no better than me are happy. Do you think I don't know what my illness is? It's boring to talk about that. Why don't they respond to love with love? I can feel their hatred day and night, even in my sleep. I think it's probably true. What frightening thoughts I have. There are lots of things you can't understand. It is I that am surprised...What are you here for? Go on talking. I cut all my connections, just like cutting off dead leaves with a pair of scissors. Now it's different. I sit and listen to the owl screeching.

TS      Nothing happened!

CO      Can't you think of a new line? That's old and stale. Do I go on living, so to speak, or do I shoot myself. Let me give a last bit of advice. Just in case, I always carry a revolver on me. See. Don't flap your hands about! Get out of the habit. All the same, I like you. Damn, it's cold. It must be time to go. I've had enough of shooting the breeze with you people. Loafing has done me in. Take yours nasty things!

*(She gathers up her belongings and moves off down the road.)*

UV      I am so happy. I have a longing for music. It's been a long time since I've played. I shall play and cry, cry like an idiot.

*(She follows **CO** off down the road.)*

S      What a glorious evening! Do you hear? How beautiful! It was all laughter, and noise, and the firing of guns…and love-making, love-making without end.

TS     Let's have some cognac. Some trash that passes for music. I'm getting plastered tonight. Drink up! There was going to be a party.

*(He moves off. **S** and **I** remain.)*

S      The angel of silence has passed over us. It's time. Goodbye. If only you knew how unwilling I am to go. My legs ache. It's as if they're made of wood. That dog's howling again.

*(**S** unexpectedly kicks **I**, knocking him off his suitcase, brutally grabs **I**'s framed dog portrait and tears off. At a loss, **I** hesitates and then follows him, running.)*

# MOVEMENT THREE

A storm is brewing. The wind is whipping through the trees. Music and laughter is heard from up the road. **CO** appears first, playfully dancing, talking and singing. One by one the characters appear on the road wearing their improvised party clothes. Suddenly, with a bolt of lightning, all the sound goes out and the party becomes macabre. They continue to laugh and talk, oblivious to the storm or to the silence. Although they are dancing, singing, and talking, there is no noise, not even the sound of their voices. As the storm escalates, the sound keeps lurching off and on. In the midst of a wild folk dance, there is another crack of lightning and abruptly they all fall to the ground. **S** sits up, desperately gasping for breath. He is reliving, for a moment, the disaster. The others, sharing his terror, are stunned. Then it is quiet again. The next moments are painfully slow and deliberate. Gradually the speed accelerates.

| | |
|---|---|
| **S** | What can I do? What can I do? Help me, help me or I'll do something stupid. |
| **TS** | It's not so bad. |
| **S** | I can't go on like this. |
| **TS** | *That's enough!* |
| **S** | I'm suffering. |
| **TS** | *Be quiet!* |
| **CO** | Before the disaster, the same thing happened. |
| **S** | What can I do? What can I do? |
| **UV** | This is agonizing. |
| **CO** | What disaster? |
| **TS** | What if we could start over. |
| **CO** | What are we to do? Tell us, what? |
| **TS** | If we could remember the life we've lived– |
| **CO** | There's no turning back. |
| **TS** | And use that as a draft, as a rough draft for another? I think that every one of us would try, more than anything else, not to repeat himself. The chief thing about each life is its pattern. Whoever loses its pattern is lost. |
| **I** | Let's have a– |
| **UV** | I want–<br>I want to–<br>I want to hear– |

| | |
|---|---|
| **I** | Let's have a game. |
| **UV** | I want to hear music. |
| **S** | Won't you try a game. |
| **UV** | I want to hear music. |
| **I** | Let's have a game. |
| **UV** | I want to hear music. |
| **S** | Won't you try a game. |
| **TS** | All right, all right! All right, ladies and gentlemen, here we go. |
| **S** | I... I...just can't go on like this. |
| **CO** | I'm going to scream. Or faint. |
| **S** | What can I do? |
| **TS** | Goddamn it, let's have a drink. |
| **S** | I... I... I... can't stay, I just can't. |
| **CO** | Have a glass of champagne. |
| **I** | I have to loosen up. |
| **UV** | Won't you have a drop of vodka. |
| **S** | Well, if you're going, go. |
| **CO** | What lovely weather we're having. |
| **S** | It wouldn't hurt to kick up your heels and have some fun. |

| | |
|---|---|
| **I** | To our good health. |
| **S** | To one who doesn't remember where she came from or why she's alive. |
| **TS** | I'm delighted to be here. |
| **UV** | I want to hear music. |
| **I** | A game of catch, dancing, or fireworks? |
| **S** | We've entered the whirlpool. |
| **I** | You head for the bright lights and spin like a top till sunrise. |
| **CO** | Dancing makes me dizzy. |
| **UV** | Plunge headlong into the abyss. |
| **S** | There it goes again. I'm dizzy. I feel sick. Help! Help! |
| **TS** | Such behavior has a bad effect on me, I get ill... |
| **CO** | Lovely weather we're having today. |
| **S** | It's not serious. I can manage on my own. |
| **CO** | Attention, please! EIN, ZWEI, DREI! |
| | *(What follows is a complex gestural/movement sequence. The characters attempt to move ahead with their brave little party but have to repeat their actions in forward and reverse sequence.)* |
| **UV** | Plunge headlong into the abyss. |
| **TS** | Well, sometimes you win and sometimes you lose. |
| **UV** | I want to talk to you. |

**TS**    Let's just make a little note of that one? What are you looking at?

**S**    Here's a riddle for you:

**CO**    Such vulgarity is beneath me.

**S**    Here's a riddle for you:

**I**    How well that dog's painted.

**TS**    Absolutely!

**I**    Yes, from life.

**CO**    Don't deceive yourself. For once in your life look truth in the eye.

**UV**    Where were you born?

**I**    I can see you have a very deep understanding of life.

**S**    I am more talented.

**CO**    You look ridiculous.

**UV**    Come and devour me.

**S**    Decadent.

**TS**    Amo, amas, amat, amamus, amatis, amant.

**UV**    One kiss.

**CO**    You'll come to a bad end.

**S**    Let me think what I want.

**CO**    What do you want?

S      Don't despair. Everything will work out. Enough now.

CO      You have completely reduced me to a state of mind.

I      I can see.

S      I am more talented.

CO      You look ridiculous.

UV      Come and devour me!

S      Decadent!

TS      Amo, amas, amat, amamus, amatis, amant.

*(Suddenly, another bolt of lightning. They all move, jerk backwards and forwards, like a needle stuck on a scratchy record. It is CO who, with great effort reaches into her pocket, takes out her little bell and rings it, a signal to the others who, freed from their stuckness, lurch forward, grabbing on to the nearest anchor.)*

TS      I can't remember the Italian for window or ceiling.

*(A sudden wind sends them spinning back to the beginning. They try again to carry, forward.)*

CO      EIN, ZWEI, DREI!

UV      Plunge headlong into the abyss.

TS      Well, sometimes you win and sometimes you lose.

UV      I want to talk to you.

TS      Let's—just make a little note of that one. What are you looking at?

S      Here's a riddle for you: morning on all fours, noon on two legs and evening on three.

| CO | Such vulgarity is beneath me. |
|---|---|
| S | Here's a riddle for you: |
| I | How well that dog's painted. Is it from life? |
| TS | Absolutely! |
| I | Yes, from life. |
| CO | Don't deceive yourself. For once in your life look truth in the eye. |
| UV | Where were you born? |
| S | Why has this man come between us? |
| UV | Where were you born? |

*(Again, a crack of lightning. Everyone is stuck, frozen in place. This time it is TS who struggles to regain movement and momentum. He struggles free and they whirl back to the beginning again.)*

| CO | EIN, ZWEI, DREI! |
|---|---|
| UV | Plunge headlong into the abyss. |
| TS | Well, sometimes you win and sometimes you lose. |
| UV | I want to talk to you. |
| TS | Well, sometimes you win and sometimes you lose. Let's just make a little note of that one. |
| UV | He's a strange person. |
| TS | Let's just make a little note of that one. What are you looking at? |

**S**      Here's a riddle for you—

**CO**    Such vulgarity is beneath me.

**S**      Here's a riddle—

**CO**    Such vulgarity is beneath me.

**S**      Here's a—

*(Again, the characters are stuck like a record skipping on a turntable. Finally S pulls himself free—)*

**S**      That was a moment of terrible desperation. I couldn't control myself, it won't happen again. It won't happen again.

*(The wind howls and sends them, once more, back to where they started.)*

**CO**    EIN, ZWEI, DREI!

**UV**    Plunge headlong into the abyss.

**TS**    Well, sometimes you win and sometimes you lose.

**UV**    You have beautiful hair.

**TS**    Well, sometimes you win and sometimes you lose.

**UV**    I want to talk to you.

**I**      I can't.

**UV**    I want to talk to you.

**I**      I can't

*(Once again the characters are forced into a jerky*

*unrelenting forwards/backwards. With great effort, **I** forces himself to stop.*)

**I**    I can't make my brains or my hands or my feet do what I want them to.

      (*Suddenly the entire little party starts to dance uncontrollably with movements that are not their own. The sound and the movement are relentless. The characters cannot stop themselves. At first they dance jerkily in counterpoint and then in frightening unison. The harder they try to stop, the more insistent the dance. Finally they act out, relive, in its entirety, the disaster from the beginning of the play. This time it is more extreme, more brutal, and toward the end it swirls around **CO** who's memory is completely activated. As the trauma subsides, all five are in a state of utter shock and recognition. **S** convulses again and bumps to a stop. **I** and **TS** wander offstage. **CO** is motionless, the memory still vibrating through her body. **UV**, who has been raped during the disaster, crawls to the picnic basket and with great difficulty opens it, rummages around and pulls out a revolver.*)

**UV**    I am going. You are my bitterest enemy. I am going mad. Am in despair. I am so unhappy. (*She points the revolver in her mouth and pulls the trigger.*) Bang! Missed. (*Now she points the revolver at **CO**.*) Missed again. BANG!

**CO**    She needs to be alone.

      (***CO** gathers her things and exits off down the road.*)

**UV**    (*Pointing the revolver at **S**.*) BANG! (*At **I**.*) BANG!

**I**    It's time you dropped it.

**UV**    Bang! Missed. Missed again. I can't stay here. Oh, what am I doing?

(*UV abruptly gathers herself and runs off disappearing down the road.*)

S      Picking up his belongings one by one. This forehead is mine, these eyes are mine, this lovely silky hair is mine. You are all mine. (*Exits.*)

I      Now I understand. (*Exits.*)

(*TS tosses his hat, following it onto the stage, his belongings strapped on his back once again. He pauses near his hat, looks in both directions, picks up his hat with his toes, tosses it gaily in the air and onto his head. His movement and voice are vaudevillian.*)

TS      What do you have against me?

(*He trots merrily off down the road, reading his book.*)

# MOVEMENT FOUR

The five reappear further down the road, walking. It is apparent that experience has altered them. They stop to take a group photograph. Since reliving the physical events of the disaster, they now remember where they have come from and what they have experienced. The quality of their speech is light and lucid, as if the words were suspended in the cool air that follows a storm.

S      What next?

TS      We'll meet again sometime. We'll hardly recognize one another. We'll say, "How do you do?" And we'll be very nervous and embarrassed. (*Takes a picture.*) Keep still... Once more, for the last time.

CO      To those who are going away! And to those who are staying! It must be time to go. There's no turning back;

the road is overgrown with weeds. It's time to go. Life goes on.

UV     When the geese have cackled, they will be still again. First they cackle and then they stop. It's been a long time since I've tasted noodles.

I     This life of ours...human life is like a flower, gloriously blooming in a meadow: along comes a goat, eats it up— no more flowers. But what am I to do? Everything!

S     I spoke so much about new forms, and now I feel myself slipping into a rut.

TS     Good-bye, trees! Good-bye, echo! Good-bye, I must go. Thank you for everything, for everything.

UV     I ought to have gone long ago. I am not responsible. I have the right to say silly things.

S     You can't let yourself go to pieces standing by the seashore waiting for the weather to turn. It's not as bad as it seems.

I     One must just struggle against all these gloomy thoughts. That's just madness.

CO     I think I know why I'm alive. Well, it doesn't matter. Paris is over and done with. That's not what makes the wheels go round. There I go again.

TS     I'm satisfied. God, I hope it all works out. I've been lucky all my life, I'm happy. People have such different fates. Something happened. I can't remember. A thousand people hoist a huge bell, loads of money and work go into the effort, and suddenly it slips and smashes to pieces. Just like that and for no reason. I've got an old-fashioned watch. It seems to be falling asleep. (*Looks at watch.*) It's about time, I think. Everything's all muddled up in my head.

**S**     You go about aimlessly in the crowd, zigzagging to and fro, you live with its life, you fuse your individuality with its, and you begin to believe that a Universal Spirit is really possible.

**I**     Take your hat and go home. I'll eat my hat before I understand anything about it. Melancholy! Anguish. Inexplicable grief. I ought to write poetry. To realize that you've outlived your time. I laughed at myself, and it seemed that the birds were laughing at me, too.

**TS**     The birds are migrating already. (*Looks up.*) Swans. Or maybe they're geese. You happy things. Here's my advise. Put on your hat, pick up your stick, and get out of here. Don't look back. And the further away you get, the better. Who's making all that noise?

**UV**     What shall I do? If only one could live the remnant of one's life in some new way. Wake up on a still sunny morning begin a new life. All the past forgotten, melted away like smoke. I ought to be going.

**CO**     *Vive la France!* We should be on our way. There's not much time. Someone here smells of herring! We're starting a new life. Yes, everything's fine now. Yes, my nerves have quieted down, that's so. On autumn evenings we'll read many books, and a new and wonderful world will open up for us. Don't worry. Here's where I head for the hills. The rest later. Marvelous weather we're having. Yes. Now we can go.

**S**     You remember me? I've got an idea. It's dull but not so bad once you're use to it. I'm going. My head is spinning! Here am I with my tremulous rays and the twinkling stars and the distant sound of a piano fainting on the perfumed air.

**UV**     I was really a little bit in love with you. I am joking, of course. *Finita la commedia.* Haven't you noticed, if you are riding through a dark wood at night and see a little light shining ahead, how you forget your fatigue and the darkness and the sharp twigs that whip your face? I suppose that in Africa the heat must be terrific now.

TS    Thank you for everything. Forgive me if things were... I talked a lot—too much, I know. Forgive me for that too, and don't think badly of me. It's time I went! Humankind is looking for something and will certainly find it. Oh, if it only happened more quickly! It's time. What? Oh, listen to the music!

I    A new life! I can't write poetry. Idleness is idleness. Weakness is weakness. I don't know any other names for them. What a queer, crazy logic. In this world everything is simple. Boots are black, sugar is sweet. I wander about my friends like a shadow. (*Clapping.*) Bravo, bravo. (*By this time I has given each of his belongings to the others. He starts to move off in the direction from which he has come, pauses, looks in the direction the group is headed.*) I feel youth waking up in me! (*Exits in the direction from which he has come.*)

S    Who's out there? Is it you? There's someone here. Do you hear the wind? What was I saying? Oh, yes... *And God help all homeless wanderers.* It's time I was on my way. What was I talking about? It isn't all the things I dreamed about, but the capacity to endure. To bear your cross and have faith. I'm no longer afraid of life. Men, lions, eagles, geese, spiders, silent fish who dwell in the deep, and those the eye cannot behold—all, all, all living things, have run their sorrowful course. (*Heads off in erratic spurts down the road until he is gone.*)

TS    And now we have to start our lives all over again... We have to go on living... There will come a time when everybody will know why, for what purpose, there is all this suffering, no more mysteries. The music is so gay, it almost seems as if a minute more, and we'd know why we live, why we suffer. If only we knew. If only we knew. (*Trots off down the road, reading, and disappears.*)

**CO**    I'll only take a minute. How odd, I can't find it any-where...Can't remember. Yes, life here is over and done with...Last year at this time it was snowing. Remember? We must be going. It's time. On our way! (*Attempts, un-successfully, to stand.*) I remember when I was six years old. Now that's what I call licking the glass clean. Good-bye to our old life. My life, my youth. I have to move on. There's not much time. We're coming. We should be on our way. It must be time to go. It's time to go. Yoohoo! It's time to go. No strength left. (*She is unable to move.*)

**UV**    We must go on living. We shall live through a long chain of days and weary evenings. We shall patiently bear the trials that fate sends us. We shall say that we have suf-fered, that we have wept, that life has been bitter to us. I see a life that is bright, lovely, beautiful. We shall rejoice and look on these troubles of ours with tenderness, with a smile—and we shall rest. I have faith. I have fervent, passionate faith. Our life will be peaceful, gentle, and sweet as a caress. You are crying. (*Walks off down the road and disappears.*)

(*CO, despondent, is left alone. She suddenly stands, picks up her belongings, walks onto the road and res-olutely faces the direction in which she must go. Slowly, heroically and with a light laugh, she lifts her parasol and begins to walk off down the road.*)

(*The last image of the play is four figures walking down the road. They each carry I's belongings. S is the last to disappear. The steady rhythm of his walking stick expresses the determination to keep going.*)

◆    ◆    ◆

# ◆ AFTERWORD ◆

Actors Theatre of Louisville and
Modern Masters—Anne Bogart

A ctors Theatre of Louisville, the State Theatre of Kentucky, has emerged as one of America's most consistently innovative professional theatre companies. For two decades it has been a major force in revitalizing American playwriting with nearly 200 ATL-premiered scripts already in publication. Its annual Humana Festival of New American Plays is recognized as the premiere event of its kind and draws producers, journalists, critics, playwrights and theatre lovers from around the world for a marathon of new works. The seasonal Classics in Context Festival is an internationally celebrated multidisciplinary event including plays, exhibits, lectures and workshops. The most recent addition to the festival lineup is Flying Solo & Friends—a unique celebration of cutting-edge performance. The biennial Bingham Signature Shakespeare offers Louisville the best of the Bard on an uncompromised production level, which only a handful of cities can achieve.

♦

Actors Theatre, under the direction of Jon Jory, is distinguished as one of the few regional companies in the country which operates three diverse theatres under one roof: the 637-seat Pamela Brown Auditorium, the 332-seat Bingham Theatre and the 159-seat Victor Jory Theatre. Its programming includes a broad range of classical and contemporary work presenting over 400 performances in a September through June season. Each play is directed and produced in Louisville with the costumes, scenery and properties seen on stage made by ATL's professional staff. Actors Theatre performs annually to over 200,000 people and is the recipient of the most prestigious awards bestowed on a regional theatre: a special Tony Award for Distinguished Achievement, the James N. Vaughan Memorial Award for Exceptional Achievement and Contribution to the Development of Professional Theatre and the Margo Jones Award for the Encouragement of New Plays. Actors Theatre's international appearances include performances in more than 29 cities in 15 foreign countries.

◆

Each year Actors Theatre of Louisville presents the Classics in Context Festival which explores the theatre of a historical/aesthetic period or individual artist through plays and a variety of multidisciplinary events. This exploration provides an opportunity to examine the social, political and aesthetic contexts within which plays were written and to celebrate important artistic movements that have shaped theatre in a number of ways. Past festivals have featured the works of Molière, Luigi Pirandello, the Moscow Art Theatre, and the French Romantics, as well as others.

For the first time during Classics in Context, Actors Theatre moved away from past, and during 1995 examined an artistic approach that directs our attention to the future, a renaissance if you will, of the American theatre as envisioned by Anne Bogart.

◆

*Events that made up the 1995 Festival:*

### PERFORMANCES

THE ADDING MACHINE by Elmer Rice; directed by Anne Bogart.

SMALL LIVES/BIG DREAMS, derived from the five major plays of Anton Chekhov. Conceived and directed by Anne Bogart with the SITI Company.

THE MEDIUM, inspired by the life and predictions of Marshall McLuhan. Conceived and directed by Anne Bogart with the SITI Company.

### KEYNOTE LECTURE

THE MEAT OF THE MEDIUM: Anne Bogart and the American Avant-Garde. Presented by Porter Anderson

## COLLOQUIA

UNDER THE INFLUENCE: Anne Bogart's Impact on Collaborators and Critics. Presented by panelists Mel Gussow, Paula Vogel and Robert Woodruff.

## POST-SHOW SYMPOSIUM

A forum for discussion amongst Anne Bogart, her casts and the audience.

## EXHIBIT

THE VIOLENT ACT OF DIRECTING, curated by Michele Volansky.

## LECTURE-DEMONSTRATION

THE VIEWPOINTS: A Movement Philosophy for the Stage, with Anne Bogart and members of the SITI Company.

## WORKSHOP

JUST DO IT!, led by members of the SITI Company.

## FESTIVAL DATES:

January 4–29, 1995

◆　　◆　　◆